Tom Snyder Productions®

Windows & Macintosh!
Versions 2000, 98, & 97!

Word Workshop
for Teachers™

by Janet Caughlin

Easy-to-Use Guide

- Create newsletters, brochures, and mail-merge letters to communicate with parents
- Use tables to create rubrics and assignment sheets
- Make prefessional looking math worksheets
- Create Web Quest sheets and Web pages

Lessons Using Word across the Curriculum

Loads of lesson ideas and templates to help meet your curriculum objectives!

Student Project Ideas

Customizable student presentations included!

Mac/Win Template CD-ROM Included!

Jam packed with sample files you can use today!

"This book is an invaluable resource for anyone using Word in the classroom."
— Jeff Ingraham
Technology Specialist, Educational Service Unit #3, Omaha, Nebraska

Copyright and Trademark Notice

Copyright

Trademarks

For more information about Tom Snyder Productions, technical help, or a free catalog, please call us at

1-800-342-0236

or visit our Web site at

www.tomsnyder.com

Limited Liability and Disclaimer of Warranty

The author and publisher have used their best efforts in preparing this book and the programs contained in it. Any information contained in this book and/or the accompanying CD-ROM, including material created by educators, students, and other third parties besides Janet Caughlin, is provided "AS IS" without any warranty of any kind. The author and publisher make no warranty of any kind, express or implied, regarding the accuracy or reliability of any information, including but not limited to the implied warranties of merchantability, fitness for a particular purpose, title, and noninfringement. Author and publisher will in no event be liable for any damages — indirect, special, incidental, or consequential — arising out of the use of, or payments based on, information or programs contained in this book. As Web sites are constantly changing, some of the Web site addresses in this book may have changed or may no longer exist. The author does not accept responsibility or liability for losses or damages resulting from information contained in this book. The author also does not support the views expressed on the Web sites contained in this book.

Acknowledgments

This book is dedicated to my family, and especially to my husband, who has been so supportive and encouraging during this project. He understands how a book takes over my life and is still willing to share in the experience after all this time.

Special acknowledgment to Diane Wolfe, who is an educator, trainer, a Microsoft® certified user, and a friend. I appreciate all the time and effort she spent helping me make this book both accurate and relevant.

Special thanks to Jeff Ingraham, Larry Wade, and Dr. George Conrad, fellow educators and trainers who shared their knowledge.

Special thanks to Marc Albert, who helped me define the book and spent hours researching and contributing to the content.

Special thanks to Matt Riley, who continues to amaze me with his skills and his willingness to help.

Thanks to Laurel Kayne, David O'Neil, and Rick Abrams for their understanding, kindness, and willingness to help.

A special thank you to the teachers who contributed their lessons to this book. They show that educators are a family that always helps one another. Thank you also to the students who contributed their files. For security reasons their names are not listed below.

Gary Schlapfer	*Fremont Middle School, Fremont, Nebraska*
Diane Johnson	*Fremont Middle School, Fremont, Nebraska*
Paula Grinvalds	*Valley Elementary School, Valley, Nebraska*
Joanne Lehman	*Clarkson Elementary School, Fremont, Nebraska*
Jan Kruse	*Fremont Elementary Schools, Fremont, Nebraska*
Ruth Follen	*Fremont Elementary Schools, Fremont, Nebraska*
Lorna McCloud	*Jackson Elementary School, Colorado Springs, Colorado*
Diane Wolfe	*Educational Service Unit #2, Fremont, Nebraska*
Sandi Snyder	*Shickley High School, Shickley, Nebraska*
Melissa Burns Johnston	*Anahuac Middle School, Anahuac, Texas*

Table of Contents

Introduction

What Is *Word* and Why Should a Teacher Want to Use It? 1
About This Book 2
Windows 95/98 Basics 4
Macintosh Basics 8
Getting Started in *Word* 13
Word Help 16
Word Toolbars 19

Learning *Word*

Word Editing Basics 25
Resume 28
Spelling and Grammar Check 31
Use the Thesaurus 34
Customize *Word* 35
Show Non-Printing Characters 40
Change the Case of Text 41
Use Comments 42
Format Painter 44
Set Tabs 45
Indent Text 46
Leader Tabs 47
Page Numbers, Headers/Footers 49
Create a Math Worksheet 51
Draw a Border 52
Bulleted Lists 55
Section Breaks 57
Decorative Characters 58
Learn About Graphics 59
Insert a Picture from a File 61
Insert a Movie 62
Internet Pictures in a Report 64
AutoShapes 65
Insert a Table 67
Footnotes 71
Leading in a Document 72
Envelopes & Labels 73
Merged Letter 74
Outline View 78
Create a Custom Outline 79
Letterheads 81
Screen Shots 84

Create a Newsletter 86

Create a Brochure 91

Create Linked Pages 95

Create a Web Page 99

How Teachers Use *Word*

Friction Lab 105

Simple Machines 106

Light Exam 107

Newton's 3 Laws 108

Temperature Notes 109

Moss/Liverwort Lab 110

Great State Lakes Activity 111

Newsletter 112

Weekly Schedule 113

Class Memory Book 114

Thanksgiving 115

Weekly Journal of Snacks for the Week 116

Examining Your School Lunch 117

Body Movement 118

FEEFE Basketball Shooting Assessment 119

"I Can" Basketball Skills Scorecard Assessment 120

Fitness Honor Roll 121

Learning Webs 122

Acrostics 123

Dear Active 124

Personal Goals 125

Multiple Intelligences 126

Lesson Plans 127

How-To Worksheets 128

Vocabulary Bingo 129

How Students Use *Word*

Community Brochure Project 133

Technical Writing Assignment 135

Kid of the Month 137

Stories That Grow 138

Tables & Vocabulary 139

Haiku Poetry 140

My Weekly Plan 141

This is *MY* Locker! 142

Primary Publishing 143

My Internet "Bug" Project 144

Christmas Around the World 145

Endangered Animal Research 146

Rainforest Research 147

Science Fair Review 148

Appendix

Word Menu Differences 151

Help! I Want to Share My *Word* File 154

Change the RAM (Memory) Allocated to *Word* 156

Animals **158**

Amphibians 158

Birds 159

Fish 163

Zoo 164

Mammals 165

Rodents 166

Reptiles 167

Insects 168

Plants **169**

Fruit, Berries, and Seeds 169

Flowers 170

Mushrooms 172

Cacti 173

Index **175**

Introduction
Detailed Contents

What Is *Word* and Why Should a Teacher Want to Use It? 1

About This Book 2
Windows and Macintosh Commands 3
Different Versions of *Word* 3
Opening Files to Complete Activities 3

Windows 95/98 Basics 4
Using the Mouse 4
Interpreting the Desktop 5
Find 6
Help 6
Shut Down 6
My Computer 6
Windows Explorer 7
Saving Files 7

Macintosh Basics 8
Using the Mouse 8
Interpreting the Desktop (Finder) 9
The Menu Bar 10
Saving Files 11

Getting Started in *Word* 13
Launching the Program 13
Creating a *Word* File 13
Opening a *Word* File 14
Saving a File 14
Printing a File 15

***Word* Help** 16
The Office Assistant 16
Button Help 17
Contents 17
Index 18
Help on the Web 18

***Word* Toolbars** 19

What Is *Word* and Why Should a Teacher Want to Use It?

Microsoft Word is the most popular word processing program in use today. Why? Maybe it's because of the incredible looking documents you can create. Or maybe it's the unique features that makes creating documents quick and easy. Using *Word*, you can create anything from simple signs and worksheets to professional-looking newsletters and brochures.

Word is a visual program, using buttons and menus to access its formatting and editing features. *Word* also provides intuitive help. For example, as you type, the program marks unknown words and grammatical errors with wavy lines. It also corrects common typos and repeats paragraph formatting. If you type "teh", *Word* will change it to "the". If you begin a paragraph with a number, e.g., 1., in the next paragraph, *Word* will type the "2." and indent as you did in the previous paragraph. Sometimes this help feature can be overwhelming for the new user, but *Microsoft* allows you to customize *Word* to meet your needs. You can turn off features and change the options and toolbars so a primary-level student or a beginning computer user can easily use the program to write a story and include graphics. Don't worry, anything you change can be changed back.

Word is also very powerful. You can hyperlink documents to other *Word* files, to *PowerPoint* presentations, *Excel* worksheets and charts, or even Web pages on the Internet. If you create a large document, like a handbook, you can insert bookmarks to hyperlink the table of contents directly to the sections and back. You can even create Web pages with *Word*.

With *Word* it's easy to insert graphics into a document. Almost any graphic, including movies and still pictures from digital cameras or scanners, can be added to your files. Visual learners in your classroom will certainly appreciate this capability.

Parts of a Flower

Petal   Stigma   Stamen

A set of drawing tools is included with *Word*. Using these tools, you can create visual worksheets and quizzes that will aid student learning and understanding.

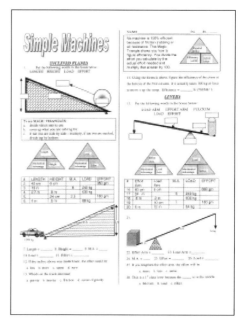

You'll find that *Word* is a tool that not only makes your job easier, it makes teaching and learning an exciting adventure!

While *Word* is easy to use, questions will still arise. *Word Workshop for Teachers* is designed to answer them for you in an easy-to-read fashion. It also contains ideas on using *Word* in the classroom.

About This Book

Word Workshop for Teachers was written by a teacher to help colleagues make better use of their valuable time. After all, who has less time and more things to do than a teacher?

This book is not a manual written in technical and hard-to-understand language. Rather, it is a guide that you can go to for help whenever the need arises. Flip through the book. You'll notice actual pictures of what should be on your computer monitor as you work through the activities. Don't worry about your typing skills; many of the activities don't require much typing. Just open a file from the CD-ROM that is included with the book and follow the step-by-step directions. If the pictures on your monitor match the ones in the book, congratulations, you've done it right! If it doesn't look quite right, go back a step or two and try it again. In no time at all, you'll be producing professional-looking documents! In each section in this book, blank note sheets are provided. This will allow you to jot down ideas or "things to try" as you go through the book.

Please note that this book assumes that you know the basics of your Windows or Macintosh computer. Though Windows and Macintosh basics are discussed briefly in this chapter, the intent of this book is to help you learn to use *Word*.

Some fellow teachers will be there to help you. Be sure to read the helpful messages next to them.

Here's how to fix it!   Don't worry if you make a mistake! Julia will tell you how to fix it. It's probably a common mistake and easy to fix!

Here's more information!   Do you need more instructions? Mary will give you more information or tell you the page where you can find a more detailed explanation.

Warning!   Read carefully whenever you see Cindy. She's a clue for you to be sure to follow the directions *exactly*!

Here's a faster way!   Todd is always in a hurry. He'll show you a faster way to do it!

Windows and Macintosh Commands

Microsoft has done a fabulous job making *Word* truly cross-platform. As a result, it is easy to include both Windows and Macintosh commands on the same page. Most things in the Windows menus are found in the Macintosh menus, though there are a few differences. Some things are found only on the Windows platform, some only on the Macintosh platform. For example, *Word 2000* on the Windows platform contains Personalized Menus. When you first start *Word 2000* only the commands that are used 95 percent of the time are visible, so infrequently used commands do not clutter the menu. At the bottom of the menu is a button to expand the menu to the full selection. If you choose a command frequently, it will be "promoted" in the list.

In this book, the Windows command is given first, followed by the Macintosh command. Screen shots are shown from both Windows and Macintosh. The similarity of the screens will allow you to work easily with either platform.

Different Versions of *Word*

This book covers the 2000 (Windows), 98 (Macintosh), and 97 (Windows) versions of *Word*. The command for 2000 is given first. If a command is different in versions 98 or 97, it is in parentheses. If a particular screen is significantly different in the three versions, all three are shown with a label identifying the version. If a feature is available only on one platform or version, you'll see this character along with an explanation.

How do you know which version of *Word* you are using?

Windows: Choose About Microsoft *Word* from the Help menu.

Macintosh: Choose About Microsoft *Word* from the Apple menu.

Word files can be opened on either a Windows or a Macintosh computer as long as files are saved on a Windows-formatted disk. The extension ".doc" needs to be added to Macintosh files so a Windows computer can read them. Versions 2000, 98, and 97 are completely compatible. See the Appendix for information about the compatibility of earlier versions.

Opening Files to Complete Activities

Many activities in this book are designed to work together with the sample files on the CD-ROM. The files on the CD-ROM are organized in folders by platform (Windows and Macintosh), then by chapter of this book. For example, the pictures below show where you would go if you were doing an activity from the chapter, Learning *Word*. You can also find graphics in the Pictures folder and movies in the Movies folder.

Windows   *Macintosh*

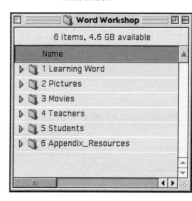

Windows 95/98 Basics

(Macintosh users turn to page 8.)

Using the Mouse

Windows computers use a mouse for many functions, including opening files and folders, accessing menus, and sizing graphics. You'll see an arrow on the computer screen. This is the cursor. The mouse moves the cursor around the screen. To use the mouse, hold it with your palm over the round end and the cord up by your fingertips. As you move the mouse, the cursor will move the same direction on the screen. If you run out of room on the mouse pad (a common problem for new users), just pick up the mouse and set it down at the other end of the mouse pad so you have more room to move.

The cursor changes shape according to what you are doing.

- If you are at the Desktop (the opening screen), the cursor is shaped like an arrow.

- If you are typing text in *Word,* the cursor is a blinking vertical line. When you move the mouse, a separate "I-beam" will move. If you click the mouse, the cursor moves to the place where the I-beam is.

- If you are in the drawing mode, the cursor is shaped like a plus sign. Spreadsheets have a fat, cross-shaped cursor.

- If the computer is doing something that takes a while, such as sorting or moving a large graphic, the cursor will change into an hourglass.

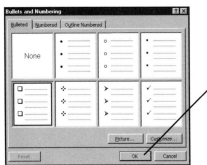

Clicking is placing the cursor on an object, pressing the mouse button down, and releasing it. Most often you click buttons, such as OK, Cancel, Open, and Save.

Double-clicking is rapidly clicking the mouse button twice, commonly done to icons, file, and disks to open or launch them.

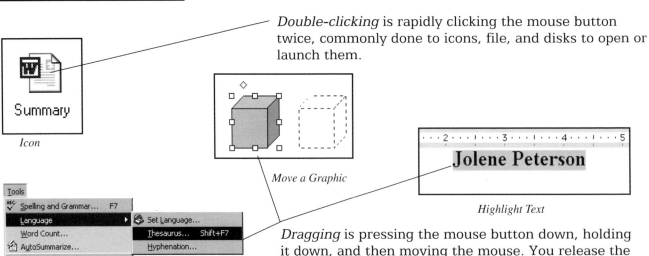

Icon

Move a Graphic

Highlight Text

Menu Option

Dragging is pressing the mouse button down, holding it down, and then moving the mouse. You release the button when you have chosen a menu option, moved a graphic to a new place, or highlighted a block of text.

Interpreting the Desktop

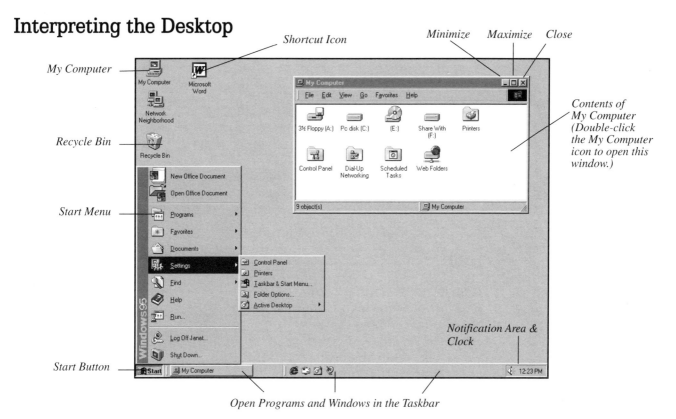

Open Programs and Windows in the Taskbar

Below is a description of the elements shown above, starting with My Computer in the upper left corner and going counterclockwise around the screen.

- **Desktop:** the screen you see when you first start the computer. Just like in your office, you can see and use the trash can, and open your files (from the hard drive).
  Note: To the layperson, the Desktop and the Finder are the same thing. The two terms are used interchangeably in this book, even though to a computer expert they are different things.

- **My Computer:** double-click to reveal the hard drive, floppy drive, CD-ROM drive, etc. Double-clicking an icon reveals the files on that drive. You can then double-click a file to open it.

- **Recycle Bin:** a trash can where you can delete things from your computer or floppy disk.

- **Start Menu:** lets you launch programs, find files and programs, and shut down the computer.

- **Start Button:** makes the Start Menu appear.

- **Taskbar:** a strip that runs along the bottom of the window. It contains very useful items, including the Start button on the left, the Open Programs and Windows area in the middle, and the Notification Area and Clock on the right. The name of programs and windows you have open appear in the middle. If you click a program/window name in the Taskbar, it moves to the front so you can use it. This allows you to move between open programs.

- **Notification Area:** shows icons that tell you what your computer is doing. A printer icon appears during printing, a speaker appears if you have a sound card, etc.

- **Close:** exits a program or closes a window.

- **Maximize:** enlarges a window to fill the screen.

- **Minimize:** makes a program disappear from the screen. You can click the program name in the Taskbar to use it again.

- **Shortcut Icons:** can be double-clicked to open files and programs.

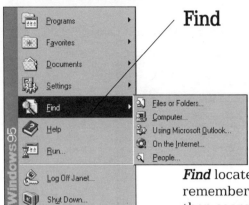

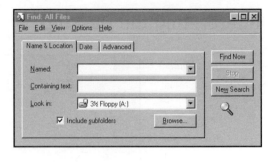

Find

Find locates files and folders. This feature is handy if you can't remember where things are. You can choose the drive(s) to search and then search by file name, the date a file was modified, or other criteria.

Help

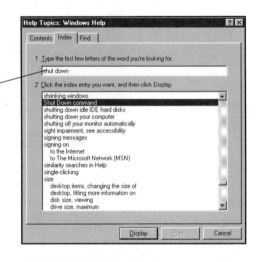

Help locates information on topics about which you want to learn more. Type the first few letters of the word you want. Then click the entry at the bottom that matches your topic. Information on that topic will appear.

Shut Down

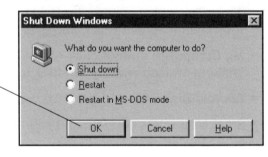

Shut Down prepares your computer to be turned off. Click the OK or Yes button, then wait until the message "You can now safely turn off your computer" appears to turn it off.

My Computer

My Computer contains icons of the hardware attached to your computer: floppy drives, hard drives, and anything else attached to your computer, e.g., a CD-ROM drive or scanner.

Windows Explorer

Windows Explorer shows you folders on your computer in a tree form. All the sub-folders and files in each folder are shown.

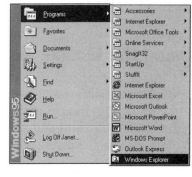

* You can open a folder and copy or move files by dragging them to the new location.

* You can create shortcuts on the desktop by dragging a file from Explorer to the desktop. This shortcut will save time in opening files. Explorer is similar to the File Manager in Windows 3.1.

The example to the right shows a Windows Explorer window.

* The left side shows the folders on the hard drive.

* The right side shows the files in the Social Studies folder (the selected one).

Saving Files

Saving a New File

When you save a new file from within a program such as *Word*, you must name the file and decide where you want it to be saved. Here are some basic instructions on how to do this.

1. Choose Save from the File menu, or press [CTRL][S].

2. Type a file name in the File Name box. Be sure the name identifies the contents of the file.

3. Click and hold down the arrow in the Save In box and navigate to the location where you want to save your file. You can choose to save on the hard drive (C:), the floppy drive (A:), or in a folder on either drive. (You can't save to the CD-ROM drive.)

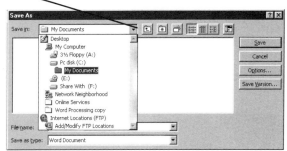

4. Click Save.

5. Once you've done this, you can simply press [CTRL][S], or choose Save from the File menu at any time to save changes to your file.

Saving a Previously Created File

This lets you save a file with another name, which is helpful if you want to change your document but preserve the original. It also enables you to save a file to a different location. For example, if you are using one of the template files on the CD-ROM that comes with this book, you will need to save the file to a location on your hard drive, since you cannot save files to a CD-ROM. Depending on the situation, you may choose to change either the file name or the location, or both. Here's how:

1. Choose Save As from the File menu.

2. Type a new file name in the Save As box. Be sure the name identifies the contents of the file.

3. Click and hold down the arrow in the Save In box at the top of the Save As window (or "dialog") and navigate to the location where you want to save your file. You can save on the hard drive (C:), the floppy drive (A:), or in a folder on either drive. (You cannot save to the CD-ROM drive.)

4. Click Save. Your old file is preserved, and you now have a new file.

Macintosh Basics

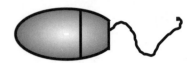

Using the Mouse

Macintosh computers use a mouse for many computer functions, including opening files and folders, accessing menus, and sizing graphics. You'll see an arrow on the computer screen. This is the cursor. The mouse moves the cursor around the screen. To use the mouse, hold it with your palm over the round end and the cord up by your fingertips. As you move the mouse, the cursor will move the same direction on the screen. If you run out of room on the mouse pad (a common problem for new users), just pick up the mouse and set it down at the other end of the mouse pad so you have more room to move. If you're using a trackball this won't even be an issue.

The cursor changes shape according to what you are doing.

- If you are at the Desktop (the opening screen), the cursor is shaped like an arrow.

- If you are typing text in *Word,* the cursor is a blinking vertical line. When you move the mouse, a separate "I-beam" will move. If you click the mouse, the cursor moves to the place where the I-beam is.

- If you are in the drawing mode, the cursor is shaped like a plus sign. Spreadsheets have a fat, cross-shaped cursor.

- If the computer is doing something that takes a while, such as sorting or moving a large graphic, the cursor will change into a watch or a spinning beach ball.

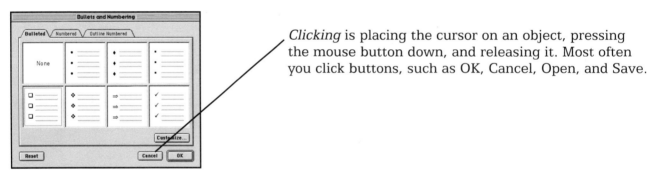

Clicking is placing the cursor on an object, pressing the mouse button down, and releasing it. Most often you click buttons, such as OK, Cancel, Open, and Save.

Double-clicking is rapidly clicking the mouse button twice, commonly done to icons, files, and disks to open or launch them.

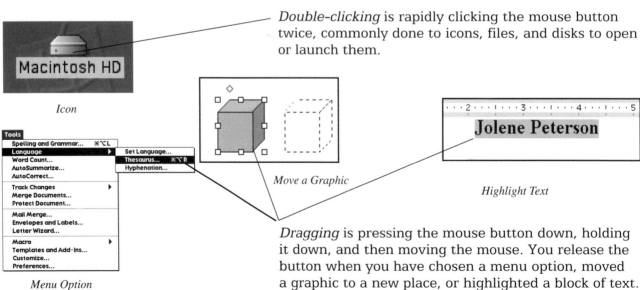

Icon

Move a Graphic

Highlight Text

Menu Option

Dragging is pressing the mouse button down, holding it down, and then moving the mouse. You release the button when you have chosen a menu option, moved a graphic to a new place, or highlighted a block of text.

Interpreting the Desktop (Finder)

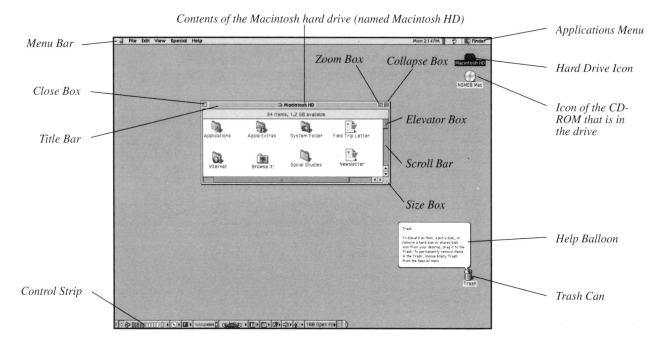

Menu Bar — *Contents of the Macintosh hard drive (named Macintosh HD)* — *Applications Menu*

Close Box — *Zoom Box* — *Collapse Box* — *Hard Drive Icon*

Title Bar — *Elevator Box* — *Icon of the CD-ROM that is in the drive*

Scroll Bar

Size Box

Help Balloon

Control Strip — *Trash Can*

- **Desktop:** the screen you see when you first start the computer. Just like in your office, you can see and use the trash can, and open your files (from the hard drive).
  Note: To the layperson, the Desktop and the Finder are the same thing. The two terms are used interchangeably in this book, even though to a computer expert they are different things.

- **Trash Can:** click and drag files to the Trash Can. Then choose Empty Trash from the Special menu to delete the contents of the trash. You can also remove disks or CD-ROMs from the computer by dragging them to the Trash Can. This does not delete any files. It just ejects the disk. ("Put Away" from the File menu does the same thing.)

- **Title Bar:** shows the name of your file or window. Click the title bar and drag it to move the window.

- **Applications Menu:** allows you to move between programs without closing them. This is a good way to see which applications are open.

- **Size Box:** click and drag this to change the size of the window.

- **Zoom Box:** lets you jump between small and large window sizes. Click in the box. Click it again. Play with the Size and the Zoom boxes. They work the same in applications like *Word*.

- **Help Balloons:** provide on-screen help as you move your cursor. To turn them on, choose Show Balloons from the Help menu. To get rid of them, choose Hide Balloons from the Help menu.

- **Scroll Arrows:** let you see files and folders inside a window. If you want to see something at the top of the window click the top arrow.

- **Elevator Box:** allows you to jump instead of scroll. Click and drag the box to a desired location, or click above or below it to jump in preset increments.

- **Close Box:** click in it to close the window.

- **Collapse Box:** lets you "roll up" windows so that only the title bar shows. Click it again to unroll the window.

The Menu Bar

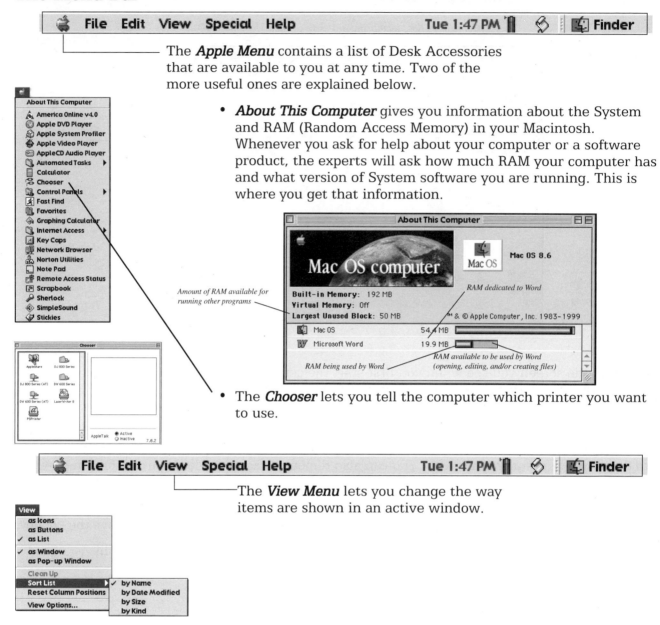

The **Apple Menu** contains a list of Desk Accessories that are available to you at any time. Two of the more useful ones are explained below.

- **About This Computer** gives you information about the System and RAM (Random Access Memory) in your Macintosh. Whenever you ask for help about your computer or a software product, the experts will ask how much RAM your computer has and what version of System software you are running. This is where you get that information.

Amount of RAM available for running other programs

RAM dedicated to Word

RAM being used by Word

RAM available to be used by Word (opening, editing, and/or creating files)

- The **Chooser** lets you tell the computer which printer you want to use.

The **View Menu** lets you change the way items are shown in an active window.

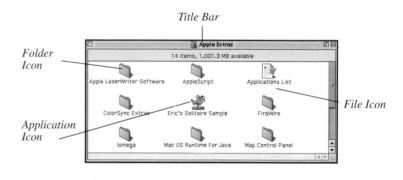

As List by Name

Title Bar

File Icon

Folder Icon

As Icons

Title Bar

Folder Icon

Application Icon

File Icon

The ***Help Menu*** gives you information about using your computer.

Help
About Help
Show Balloons
Help   ⌘?

- ***About Help*** teaches you to use the Macintosh Help system.

- ***Show Balloons*** gives you on-screen help balloons. As you move the cursor, balloons appear with explanations about the items the cursor touches. Hide Balloons turns them off. Hide Balloons appears in the menu only after you select Show Balloons.

- ***Help*** starts the Mac OS Help system. The system has a complete index of topics relating to the use and customization of your Macintosh.

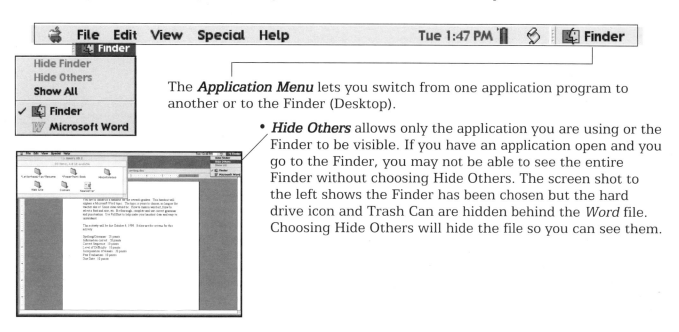

The ***Application Menu*** lets you switch from one application program to another or to the Finder (Desktop).

- ***Hide Others*** allows only the application you are using or the Finder to be visible. If you have an application open and you go to the Finder, you may not be able to see the entire Finder without choosing Hide Others. The screen shot to the left shows the Finder has been chosen but the hard drive icon and Trash Can are hidden behind the *Word* file. Choosing Hide Others will hide the file so you can see them.

Saving Files

Saving a New File
When you save a new file, you must tell the computer the name of the file and where you want it to be saved.

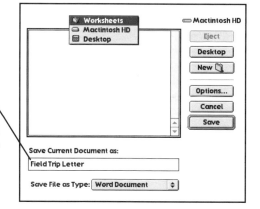

1. Choose Save from the File menu, or press ⌘S.

2. Type a file name in the Save As box. Be sure the name identifies the contents of the file.

3. Click the pull-down menu at the top of the dialog box, and then navigate to the location where you want to save your file. You can choose to save on the hard drive, a floppy disk, or in a folder in either of these places. (You can't save to a CD-ROM.)

4. Click Save.

5. Once you've done this, you can simply press ⌘S, or choose Save from the File menu at any time to save changes to your file.

Saving a Previously Created File

This lets you save a file with another name, which is helpful if you want to change your document but preserve the original. It also enables you to save a file to a different location. For example, if you are using one of the template files on the CD-ROM that comes with this book, you will need to save the file to a location on your hard drive, since you cannot save files to a CD-ROM. Depending on the situation, you may choose to change either the file name or the location, or both. Here's how:

1. Choose Save As from the File menu.

2. Type a new file name in the Save As box. Be sure the name identifies the contents of the file.

3. Click the pull-down menu at the top of the dialog box and navigate to the location where you want to save your file. You can choose to save on the hard drive, a floppy disk, or in a folder in either location. (You can't save to a CD-ROM.)

4. Click Save. Your old file is preserved, and you now have a new file.

Getting Started in *Word*

Word is part of a suite of programs called Microsoft *Office*, so it is usually found in a folder called Microsoft Office. Below are instructions on how to launch the program (also called an application) and do some basic things to get you started. You will need to be familiar with these basics to do the activities in the Learning *Word* section.

Launching the Program

Windows

Here are two ways to launch the program:

- Your computer may have shortcuts to programs on the desktop. If so, **double-click** the Microsoft *Word* **shortcut** to launch the program.

- Or click **Start** in the lower left corner of the desktop. Then drag up to **Programs,** and **drag right and down** to select Microsoft *Word.*

Microsoft Word Shortcut on Windows

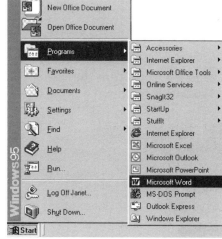

Macintosh

Here are two ways to launch the program:

- Your computer may have a set of aliases to programs on the desktop. If so, **double-click** the Microsoft *Word* **alias** to launch the program.

- Or locate the actual program on the hard drive and **double-click** the Microsoft *Word* icon.

Word Alias on Macintosh

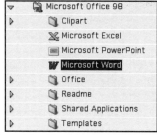

Launching Word from program icon

Creating a *Word* File

This is the screen you'll see if you open Microsoft *Word* using one of the methods above. You'll be ready to start typing a new document.

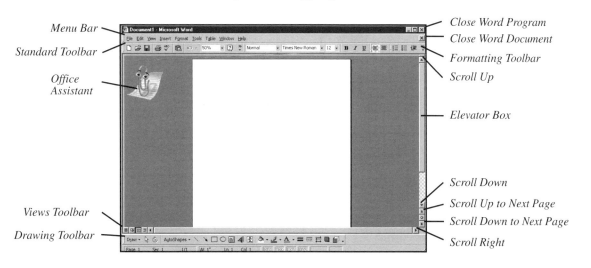

Creating a *Word* File from within the Program

Here's how to create a new file if you have already started *Word*.

1. Click the **New** icon

   or

   press [CTRL][N] (Windows) [⌘][N] (Macintosh)

   to get a new *Word* file.

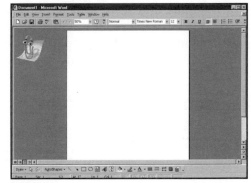

2. Choose **New** from the **File** menu to see more choices. You can click the tabs, e.g., **Letters and Faxes** tab, to open a template.

Anytime you see what looks like a file folder tab, you can click on any one and it will display its contents.

Opening a *Word* File

There are three ways to open a file.

- Click the **Open** icon on the toolbar

   or

- choose **Open** from the **File** menu

   or

- press [CTRL][O] (Windows) [⌘][O] (Macintosh).

From there, navigate to the file you wish to open and double-click it.

Note: *Word* will open files from all earlier versions of the program. If you don't see the file you want to open, choose All Files from "Files of type" at the bottom of the window (called "List files of Type" on Macintosh). You must do this to open files saved as templates, outlines, or Web pages.

Saving a File

Saving a *Word* file works just like saving a file in any word processing program.

1. Click the **Save** icon on the toolbar

   or

   choose **Save** from the **File** menu

   or

   press [CTRL][S] (Windows) [⌘][S] (Macintosh).

2. Name your file.

3. Navigate to where you want to save the file.

4. Click **Save.**

Note: If you want people with earlier versions of *Word* to be able to open your file, you need to use the drop-down menu next to the words **"Save as type"** ("Save File as Type" on Macintosh) and select the appropriate version.

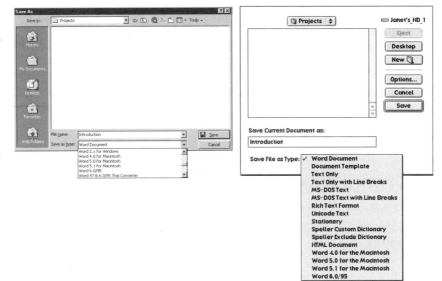

For more detailed instructions on saving files, see page 7 for Windows and pages 11–12 for Macintosh.

Printing a File

The basics of printing a *Word* file are easy. Simply do one of the following:

- Click the **Print** icon on the toolbar

   or

- choose **Print** from the **File** menu

   or

- press [CTRL][P] (Windows) [⌘][P] (Macintosh).

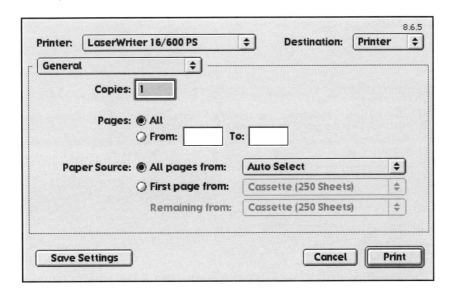

Word Help

One of the best things about *Word* is its built-in help features. If you are in the middle of something and can't figure out how to finish it, you can ask the Office Assistant by clicking its button (or pressing F1 on Windows). You can also access the Help menu and dig deeper into a topic using Contents, Index, or Find. These options are found in both *Word 97* and *Word 2000* on the Windows platform and *Word 98* on the Mac. As you browse these pages, you'll see there are many similarities and only a few differences in the help features for Windows and Macintosh.

The Office Assistant

The Office Assistant is a quick way to access help. If you are in the middle of a procedure and you're not sure what to do next, ask the Assistant. **You can also type your question and click Search.** The Assistant will present a list of topics. Click the blue button next to your chosen topic or redefine your question.

If the Office Assistant isn't visible, you can access it by clicking the Assistant button on the Toolbar.
On Windows, you can also press F1.

To hide the Assistant, right-click the Assistant (Control-click for Macintosh) and then click Hide Assistant.

If you don't want the Assistant to guess which Help topics you want, right-click the Assistant (Control-click for Macintosh), and then click Options. On the Options tab, clear the Guess Help topics check box.

Clicking the button next to the word **Tip** or clicking the **light bulb** (if it appears) gives you a **tip for the day.**

Macintosh

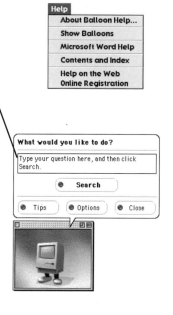

Windows

Here's a trick: *If you don't like the "Paperclip Face" or "Computer Face" Assistant, **you can choose another face!** Right-click the Assistant (or Control-click on Macintosh), and then click Choose Assistant. On the Gallery tab, click Next or Back until you find an Assistant you like!*

Button Help

If you are using a Windows computer you can press Shift F1 to access Help. The cursor will change to an arrow and a question mark. Click a button to see what it does. When you click, an explanation window appears.

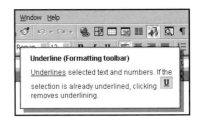

Contents

Additional help can be accessed by clicking the **Help** menu and choosing **Contents and Index**. The first tab, **Contents**, gives you a detailed list of help topics. It is arranged in an outline format, with book icons indicating major topics. Clicking or double-clicking a book will reveal sub-topics.

A closed book has topics hidden behind it. Double-click (single-click on a Macintosh) to open and the hidden sub-topics will drop below it.

Windows

Macintosh

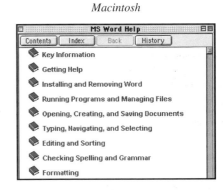

An open book contains topics as well as closed books.

Double-click a book and then double-click a topic to obtain information. On a Macintosh computer, click once to see an explanation window.

Click an arrow to get additional information.

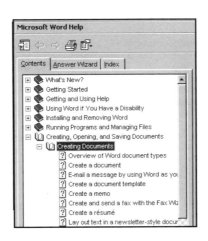

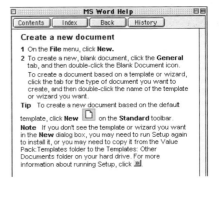

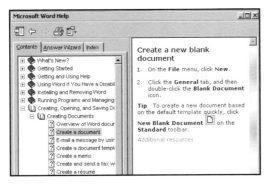

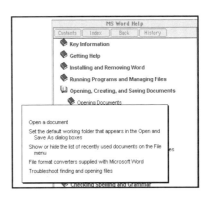

Index

Additional help can be accessed by clicking the **Help** menu and choosing **Contents and Index**. The second tab or button, **Index**, gives you a detailed list of help topics and also allows you to type in a topic. This format is helpful if you can't think of an exact topic and are guessing.

Click the **Index** tab or button. Type a topic to narrow your search. Sub-topics will appear in a separate box. Double-click (single-click for Macintosh) a topic to see detailed information.

Windows   *Macintosh*

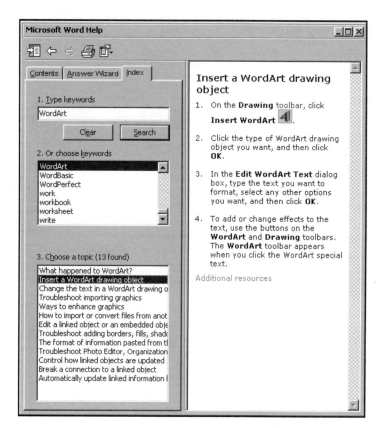

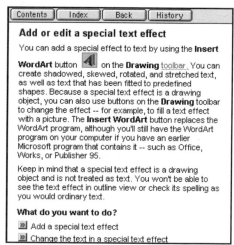

Anytime you see what looks like a file folder tab, you can click on any one and it will display its contents.

Help on the Web

Online help (such as updates, templates, etc.) from Microsoft is available on the Microsoft Web site. If you choose **Office on the Web** from the **Help** menu (**Help on the Web** for Macintosh), *Word* will attempt to connect to this site via your browser. If this doesn't work, launch your browser and try the command again. If you still don't succeed, you can always type the Microsoft URL directly into your browser: http://microsoft.com

Windows   *Macintosh*

Word Toolbars

Word lets you click a button on a toolbar to perform a task. You can also use menu commands, but you may find it faster to click a button on the toolbar. For example, you can click the Save icon or click the File menu, then drag to the Save command. Try both methods and see which one appeals to you.

Standard Toolbar

Word 2000

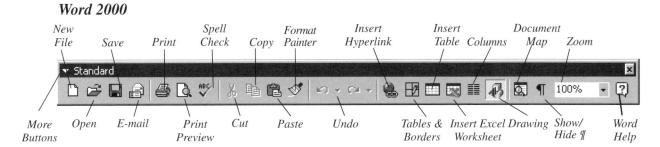

New File · Save · Print · Spell Check · Copy · Format Painter · Insert Hyperlink · Insert Table · Columns · Document Map · Zoom

More Buttons · Open · E-mail · Print Preview · Cut · Paste · Undo · Tables & Borders · Insert Excel Worksheet · Drawing · Show/Hide ¶ · Word Help

Word 98 & 97

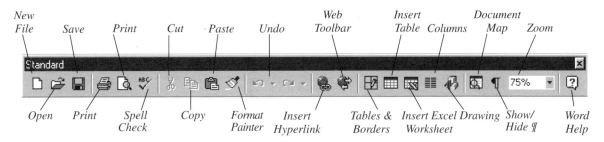

New File · Save · Print · Cut · Paste · Undo · Web Toolbar · Insert Table · Columns · Document Map · Zoom

Open · Print · Spell Check · Copy · Format Painter · Insert Hyperlink · Tables & Borders · Insert Excel Worksheet · Drawing · Show/Hide ¶ · Word Help

Formatting Toolbar

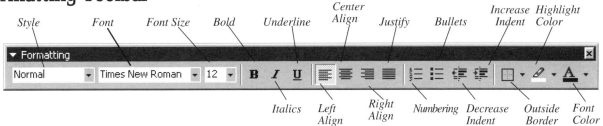

Style · Font · Font Size · Bold · Underline · Center Align · Justify · Bullets · Increase Indent · Highlight Color

Italics · Left Align · Right Align · Numbering · Decrease Indent · Outside Border · Font Color

If you can't find a toolbar on your screen, click the View menu, drag to choose Tools, then click the toolbar you need.

Views Toolbar

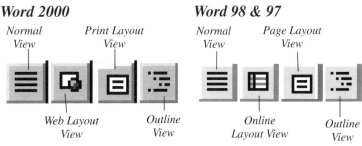

Word 2000

Normal View · Print Layout View

Web Layout View · Outline View

Word 98 & 97

Normal View · Page Layout View

Online Layout View · Outline View

WordArt Toolbar

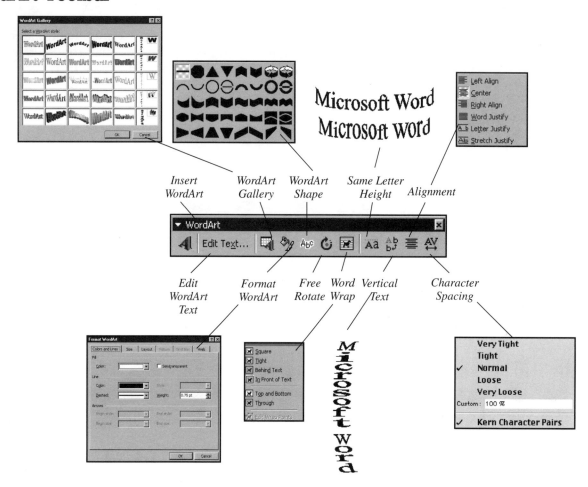

Web Toolbar

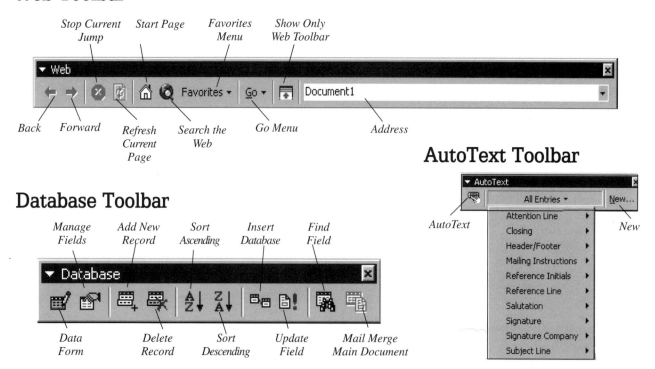

Database Toolbar

AutoText Toolbar

Drawing Toolbar

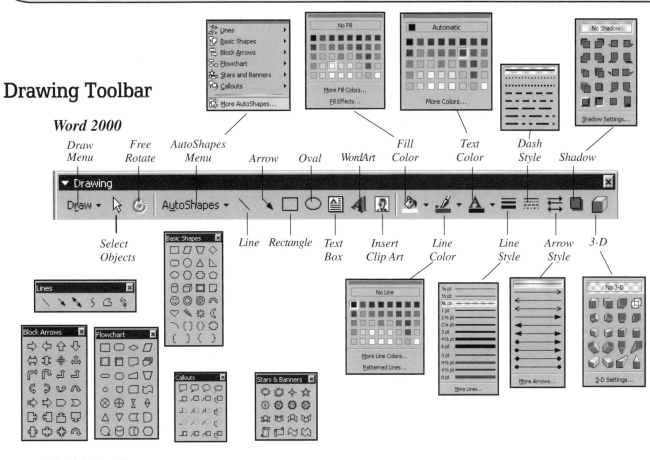

Word 98 & 97

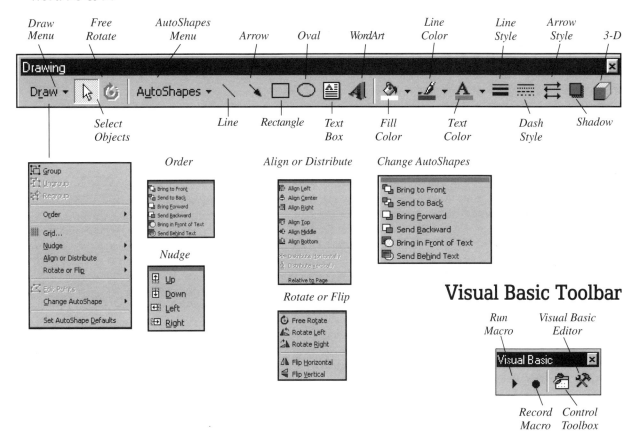

Visual Basic Toolbar

Picture Toolbar

Word 2000

Insert Picture from File · More Contrast · More Brightness · Crop · Text Wrapping · Transparent Color

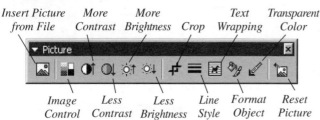

Image Control · Less Contrast · Less Brightness · Line Style · Format Object · Reset Picture

Word 98 & 97

Insert Picture from File · More Contrast · More Brightness · Crop · Text Wrapping · Transparent Color

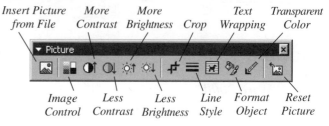

Image Control · Less Contrast · Less Brightness · Line Style · Format Object · Reset Picture

Detailed menus are shown in the Appendix.

Tables & Borders Toolbar

Draw Table · Eraser · Border Style · Border Width · Border Color · Shading Color · Merge Cells · Align Cells · Distribute Columns Evenly · Change Text Direction · Sort Descending

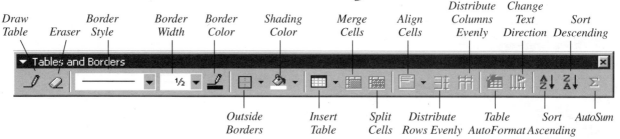

Outside Borders · Insert Table · Split Cells · Distribute Rows Evenly · Table AutoFormat · Sort Ascending · AutoSum

Frames Toolbar

Table of Contents in Frame · New Frame Left · New Frame Right · New Frame Above · New Frame Below · Delete Frame · Frame Properties

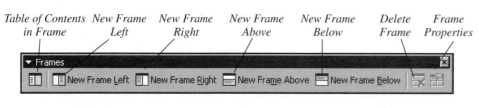

Shadow Toolbar

Shadow On/Off · Nudge Down · Nudge Right

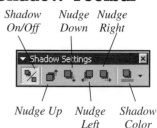

Nudge Up · Nudge Left · Shadow Color

Reviewing Toolbar

Insert Comment · Previous Comment · Delete Comment · Previous Change · Accept Change · Highlight Color · Save Version

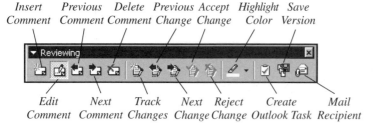

Edit Comment · Next Comment · Track Changes · Next Change · Reject Change · Create Outlook Task · Mail Recipient

3-D Settings Toolbar

3-D On/Off · Tilt Up · Tilt Right · Direction · Surface

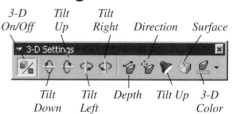

Tilt Down · Tilt Left · Depth · Tilt Up · 3-D Color

Forms Toolbar

Text Form Field · Drop-down Form Field · Draw Table · Insert Frame · Protect Form

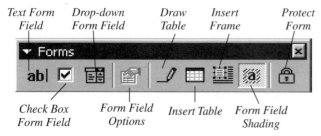

Check Box Form Field · Form Field Options · Insert Table · Form Field Shading

Control Toolbox Toolbar

Properties · Check Box · Command Button · List Box · Toggle Button · Scroll Bar · Image

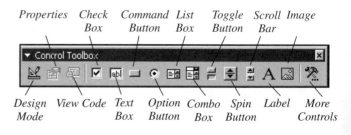

Design Mode · View Code · Text Box · Option Button · Combo Box · Spin Button · Label · More Controls

Learning *Word*

Detailed Contents

Word Editing Basics
A Sample Field Trip Letter 25

Resume
Create a Great Resume 28

Spelling and Grammar Check
Learn to Check Spelling and Grammar 31

Use the Thesaurus
Learn to Use the Thesaurus 34

Customize *Word*
Make *Word* Easier for Beginners 35

Show Non-Printing Characters
Now You Can See How Things Happen 40

Change the Case of Text
Make *Word* Correct Your Capitalization Errors 41

Use Comments
Use Comments to Give Feedback on Papers 42

Format Painter
Jazz Up a Worksheet 44

Set Tabs
Learn to Create a Schedule 45

Indent Text
Make a List That Wraps 46

Leader Tabs
Create a Short Answer Test 47

Page Numbers, Headers/Footers
Put Automatic Page Numbers in a Document 49

Create a Math Worksheet
Make a Fractions Worksheet for Your Class 51

Draw a Border
Make a Classroom Rules Poster 52

Bulleted Lists
Create Supplies Checklists 55

Section Breaks
Insert an Outline in Part of a Document 57

Decorative Characters
Give Your Text a Formal Look 58

Learn About Graphics
Understand How Graphics Work 59

Insert a Picture from a File
Create a Graphic Study Guide 61

Insert a Movie
Create a Self-Study Sheet with a Movie 62

Internet Pictures in a Report
Create a Worksheet with Internet Pictures 64

AutoShapes
Use AutoShapes in Your Documents 65

Insert a Table
Create a Rubric and an Assignment Sheet 67

Footnotes
Use Footnotes in a Letter 71

Leading in a Document
Tighten Up the Text 72

Envelopes & Labels
Create Envelopes the Easy Way 73

Merged Letter
Merge Names & Addresses in a Letter 74

Outline View
Create an Outline 78

Create a Custom Outline
Create an Outline That Exactly Meets Your Needs 79

Letterheads
Create Your Own Stationery 81

Screen Shots
Create a Computer Worksheet 84

Create a Newsletter
Send a Newsletter Home Every Week 86

Create a Brochure
Create a Great-Looking Informational Brochure 91

Create Linked Pages
Create an Interactive Activity 95

Create a Web Page
Create an Animals Web Page 99

Word Editing Basics

A Sample Field Trip Letter

Microsoft *Word* is easy to learn. This activity takes you though a quick tour of a *Word* document and shows you how to make frequently used edits.

> ### This Activity Covers the Following Topics
> - Editing text
> - Formatting text
> - Setting tabs
> - Justifying the text
> - Previewing the document
> - Inserting a letterhead
> - Drawing a rectangle in the letterhead
> - Saving the file
> - Printing the file

Editing Text

1. Open the file "Field Trip Letter" on the CD-ROM that came with this book.

2. **Double-click** the word "**kids**" in the first line. The entire word will become highlighted. Type the word "**students,**" but *don't press the delete key first*. Notice that as you start typing, the word "kids" is deleted and replaced with "students."

3. Click *immediately* **after the word "animal"** in the second line in the sentence reading "They have researched where animal live..." **Type** the letter "**s**" to make the word plural.

4. Click *immediately* **after the word "family"** in the next line. This also needs to be plural. Press the **Backspace** key (**Delete** for Macintosh) to erase the "**y**" and **type** "**ies.**"

Formatting Text

1. The places toured by the students will be easier to see if they are emphasized. You're going to italicize this text. Click in front of the **"L"** in **Lied Jungle**. Hold down [SHIFT] and click the mouse after the second **"o"** in the word **Zoo**. This highlights everything between the click and the shift-click ("Lied Jungle at the Henry Doorly Zoo" in this case). This is the *Click Shift-Click* method of highlighting text.

2. Click the **Italic** button *I* on the toolbar at the top of the screen

   or

   press [CTRL][ ] (Windows) [⌘][ ] (Macintosh)

   or

   choose **Font** and then click **Italics** from the **Format** menu, then click **OK**.

3. Using the Click Shift-Click method, **italicize Gifford Farm.**

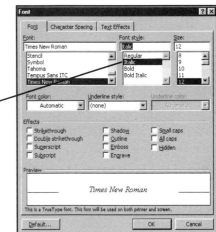

4. Scroll down until all the activities for the field trip are visible on your screen. **Double-click** "**Activity.**" **Boldface** and **underline** the word. Then boldface and underline the words "**Begin**" and "**Leave.**" **Hint:** You can make both changes in quick succession.

Click the boldface button **B** then the underline button **U**

or

press [CTRL][B] then [CTRL][U] (Windows) [⌘][B] then [⌘][U] (Macintosh)

or

choose **Font,** then **Bold,** and then **Underline** from the **Format** menu.

Setting Tabs

1. Click in front of the "**L**" in the word "**Load**" under the heading **Activity.** While holding the mouse button, drag the mouse down and to the right to select (highlight) the entire schedule.

2. Click the **1/2"** mark on the ruler. This will insert a **Left** justified **tab** at that location **L**.

3. You can change the type of tab you insert by clicking the **Tab Box** button to the left of the ruler. Click the button **twice** to choose a right justified tab **⬛**. You'll learn more about tabs on page 45.

4. Click the **4 1/2"** and **5 1/2"** marks on the ruler to insert **Right** justified tabs at those locations.

5. Place the "**I-beam**" to the **left** of the "**8**" in **8:30** on the first line of the activities. **Click** to move the cursor to that location. **Press** [TAB]. "8:30" will move to the right under "Begin." **Tab the rest of the activities.** Press the Tab key two times for the lines that include a time to leave (Arrive at zoo and Leave Gifford Farm).

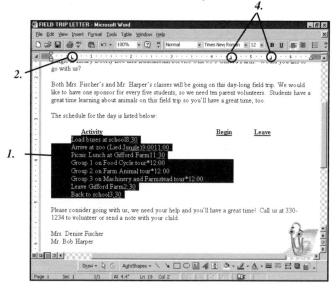

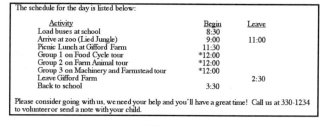

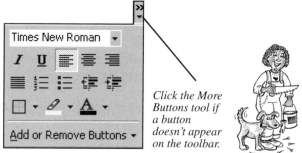

Click the More Buttons tool if a button doesn't appear on the toolbar.

Justifying the Text

Choose **Select All** from the **Edit** menu or **press** Ca (Windows) Ua (Macintosh) to highlight the entire document. Click the **Justify Text** button to justify the letter. **▤**

Previewing the Document

1. Choose **50%** from the **Zoom Box** [50% ▾] The letter appears on the screen reduced to 50% of its original size. You can see that only two-thirds of the page is taken up by the letter. This will allow a letterhead to be inserted at the top.

2. Choose **100%** from the **Zoom Box.**

3. Type the **current year** in the date. **Click** to the **left of the M** in **May**. **Press** [ENTER] (Windows) [RETURN] (Macintosh) **seven times** to move the text down the page.

Inserting a Letterhead

1. **Click the "I-Beam" two lines down from the top margin**. Click the **Center Text** button ☰.

2. Click the **Bold** button or **press** [CTRL][B] (Windows) [⌘][B] (Macintosh) to boldface the text you are about to type.

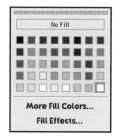

Mrs. Denise Fischer
Mr. Bob Harper
Valley Public Schools

May 2, ----

3. Choose "**24 Point**" from the **Size** menu. `Times ▾ 24 ▾`

4. Type the letterhead text shown above or type your name, a colleague's name, and your school name. Press [ENTER] (Windows) [RETURN] (Macintosh) at the end of each line, (text will be centered, 24 point, and bold because you just chose those text formatting options).

5. **Click to the left of the "M" in Mrs. Denise Fischer** (or the first name that you typed). **Press** [ENTER] (Windows) [RETURN] (Macintosh) once to move the line down the page.

Drawing a Rectangle in the Letterhead

1. Choose the **Rectangle** tool from the **Drawing** toolbar `Draw ▾ ⬏ ↻ AutoShapes ▾ ＼ ↘ ☐`. Starting at the upper left corner, draw a rectangle around the 3 lines containing the teachers and school names. The text will disappear behind the filled-in square. (Don't panic!)

2. Choose **Order**, then **Send Behind Text** from the **Draw** menu at the bottom of the screen `Draw ▾`. Your words will reappear!

3. Choose a **Fill Color** from the **Fill Color** icon `🎨▾` in the **Drawing** toolbar. The box fills with that color.

4. **Click somewhere in the letter to deselect the square**. (The small squares or handles on the corners disappear.)

5. **Draw another rectangle outside of the first one.** Again, it covers the text. This time instead of moving the rectangle behind the text you're going to make it transparent.

6. Choose **No Fill** from the **Fill Color palette.** The text and the previous box appear because the new box is now transparent.

7. Choose **50%** from the **Zoom Box**. The letter appears on the screen reduced to 50% of its original size. If you need to make any changes, you can make them in this size or return to a larger size using the Zoom Box.

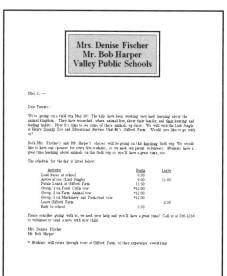

Saving the File

You did it! Choose **Save As** from the **File** menu, to save your file. Save it on your hard drive or floppy disk.

Printing the File 🖨

Click the **Print** button, choose **Print** from the **File** menu, or **press** [CTRL][P] (Windows) [⌘][P] (Macintosh) to print your file.

Resume

Create a Great Resume

You should keep your resume updated because you never know when you'll need to use it. Resumes aren't just for jobs, they are also needed if you apply for a grant or honor. *Word* makes it easy to create professional-looking resumes and the directions below will show you how.

This Activity Covers the Following Topics
- Selecting, Boldfacing, and Changing the Size of Text
- Changing Margins, Setting Tabs
- Showing Non-Printing Characters
- Indenting Text
- More Tabs
- Finding and Changing Text
- Drawing Lines for Emphasis
- Previewing the Document
- Saving the File
- Creating a Resume Using the Wizard

Selecting, Boldfacing, and Changing the Size of Text

1. Open the file "Resume" from the CD-ROM that came with this book.

2. Select the name **Jolene Peterson** on the top line.

3. Click the **Bold** button **B**

    or

    Press **CTRL B** (Windows) **⇧⌘B** (Macintosh)

    or

    Choose **Font,** then **Bold** from the **Format** menu.

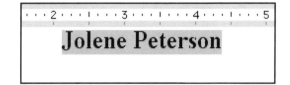

4. Choose **24** from the **Font Size** box **24 ▾**.

5. Click the **Center** button **≡**.

6. Continuing down the page, select and **boldface** the titles **Career Objective, Employment Experience, Related Experiences, Sponsored:, Coaching:, Education, Professional Organizations.**

Changing Margins, Setting Tabs

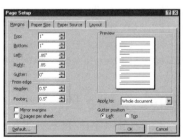

1. Choose **Page Setup** from the **File** menu (98 users choose **Document** from the **Format** menu). In the **Margins** tab, select the "1" in the box next to the word "**Left.**" Type "**.85**" to change the left margin from 1" to .85". Press the **Tab** key and do the same on the **right** margin. **Click OK.**

2. Select the **address and phone number lines.** These lines need tabs to set the information apart in an attractive manner. Click a **left tab** at **2 3/4"**. Set a **right tab** close to the **right margin marker.** Turn to the Setting Tabs section of the previous activity for help on setting tabs.

3. Click in front of the "**P**" in the word "**Phoenix**" in the first address line and press ⟦TAB⟧. **Click** in front of the "**H**" by the **home phone** number and press ⟦TAB⟧. **Do the same in the second line**.

Jolene Peterson

204 Park Avenue South	Phoenix, Arizona 50326	H 602-559-2654
401 South 147 Street	Phoenix, Arizona 50326	W 602-843-4587

Showing Non-Printing Characters

1. Click the **Show/Hide Non-Printing Characters** button ¶. Formatting characters will appear. The same command will hide the characters. A "•" appears between each word to show the Spacebar was pressed. An arrow → indicates the Tab key was pressed, and ¶ means ⟦ENTER⟧ (Windows) ⟦RETURN⟧ (Macintosh) was pressed.

Jolene Peterson¶

204 Park Avenue South	→	Phoenix, Arizona 50326	→	H 602-559-2654	¶
401 South 147 Street	→	Phoenix, Arizona 50326	→	W 602-843-4587	¶

2. The text under the headings **Employment Experience** and **Related Experiences** need tabs set into the ruler to align it in a readable and attractive manner. **Select all the text under these headings**. The non-printing characters show you the tab key was pressed when the file was created, but the tabs are no longer in the ruler. This was done so you can see how the tabs affect the document when they are put in the ruler. You don't have to spend time pressing the tab key.

   Click the **Show/Hide Non-Printing Characters** button ¶ to hide the characters.

3. Click a **left tab** at **1"**. As discussed in the previous step, the text will move because the Tab key was pressed when the file was created.

Indenting Text

The Related Experiences section would look much better if the second lines of multi-line experiences are indented so they line up on the tab.

1. Select the text under **Related Experiences** again.

2. Drag the **bottom triangle** (Hanging Indent marker) of the left margin marker on top of the tab you set in the last step. The indent marker has two parts. The △ affects the position of text that wraps to the next line. The ▽ affects the position of the first character. (You'll learn more about hanging indents on page 46.)

   The text that wrapped to a second line will be indented (lined up) on the indent marker.

More Tabs

The Sponsored and Coaching sections need tabs to improve their readability and appearance.

1. **Select** the headings and text under "**Sponsored**: **Coaching**:." Click a **left tab** at **3"**.

2. **Select** the headings and text under **Education Professional Organizations**. Set **left tabs** at **3/4"** and **3 1/2"**.

Finding and Changing Text

1. To change the name on the resume, select **Replace** from the **Edit** menu or **press** ⟦CTRL⟧⟦H⟧ (Windows) ⟦⌘⟧⟦H⟧ (Macintosh).

2. A dialog box appears. Type "**Jolene Peterson**" in the **Find what** box. Press the **Tab** key. Type **your name** in the **Replace with** box.

3. Click the **Find Next** button. The computer will find the name. If the dialog box covers up the name, click and drag on the dark or striped title bar to move the box so you can see behind it.

When the computer selects the name Jolene Peterson, click the **Replace** button. It will replace Jolene's name with yours!

4. Click the **Find Next** button to see if there are any other occurrences of Jolene's name. When there are no others, click **Close.**

Drawing Lines for Emphasis

1. Scroll to the **top of your document**.

2. Choose the **Straight Line** tool from the **Drawing** toolbar .

3. Hold down SHIFT and **drag the cursor** just above the address lines to draw a line from margin to margin. The Shift key forces a straight line. Release the mouse button before the Shift key. Do the same below the address lines. **Note:** Use the arrows on the keyboard to move the line up and down as needed.

Previewing the Document

1. *Word* gives you another way to zoom in on your file. Choose **Print Preview** from the **File** menu so you can see the entire document.

2. Click **Close**.

Saving the File

1. Great! Choose **Save As** from the **File** menu and save it on your hard drive or floppy disk.

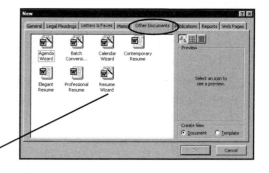

Creating a Resume Using the Wizard

1. Choose **New** from the **File** menu or press CTRL N (Windows) ⌘ N (Macintosh).

2. Click the **Other Documents** tab. Three resume templates are available as well as the Resume Wizard.

3. Double-click **Resume Wizard.**

4. Click **Next**. Then choose a resume **Type**, then a **Style**. Don't worry, you can choose a different style later.

5. Keep clicking **Next** and entering information as the Wizard takes you through the steps.

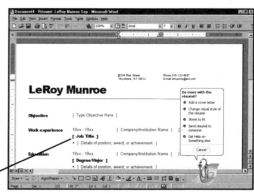

6. The personal information you type in is entered into the resume. The headings you chose, e.g., **Objective**, appear with spaces enclosed by brackets "[ ]" for you to enter your data. Enter your data and preview the finished resume by clicking **Finish.**

7. Let the Wizard show you the resume in all three styles.

Spelling and Grammar Check

Learn to Check Spelling and Grammar

Spelling and grammar checkers will never replace our brains, but they can help us find many mistakes. This activity will show you how to use the spelling and grammar checkers in *Word*.

This Activity Covers the Following Topics
- Checking Spelling
- Checking Grammar

Checking Spelling

1. Open the file "Spell Check Assign" from the CD-ROM that came with this book. Words that the spell checker doesn't recognize have a wavy red line under them. Grammatical errors have a wavy green line.

2. Right-click the misspelled word "buton" at the beginning of the fourth line (Macintosh users [CTRL] click) and choose the correct spelling.

3. Click the **Spell Check** button ✓ or choose **Spelling and Grammar** from the **Tools** menu (Windows users can also press F7). Use the commands below to check the document. Use the commands on the next page to check the grammar.

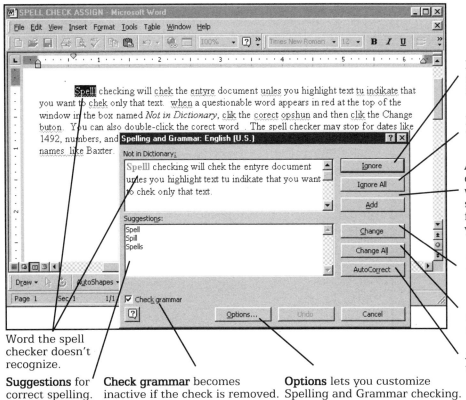

Ignore the spell checker suggestions because the word is spelled correctly.

Ignore All suggestions because the word is spelled correctly.

Add this word to the user dictionary so the spell checker will recognize it as a correctly spelled word. Use this feature for names and unusual words you use frequently.

Change the unknown word to the selected suggestion or double-click the correct spelling.

Change All words spelled this way to the selected suggestion.

AutoCorrect lets you add a selected word to the AutoCorrect list.

Word the spell checker doesn't recognize.

Suggestions for correct spelling.

Check grammar becomes inactive if the check is removed.

Options lets you customize Spelling and Grammar checking.

Checking Grammar

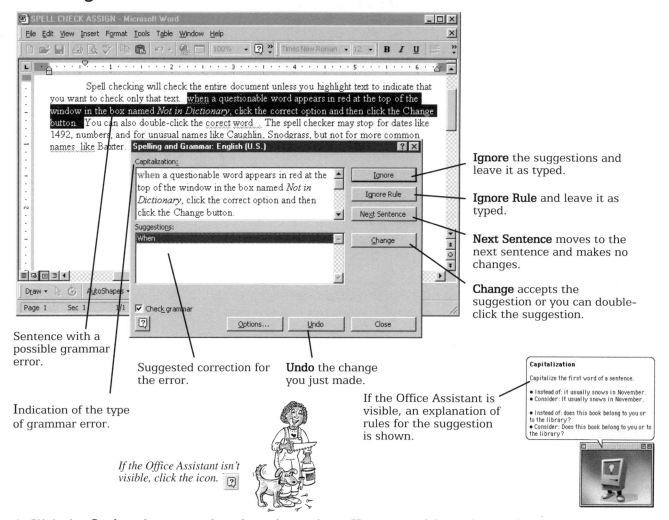

Ignore the suggestions and leave it as typed.

Ignore Rule and leave it as typed.

Next Sentence moves to the next sentence and makes no changes.

Change accepts the suggestion or you can double-click the suggestion.

Sentence with a possible grammar error.

Suggested correction for the error.

Undo the change you just made.

If the Office Assistant is visible, an explanation of rules for the suggestion is shown.

Indication of the type of grammar error.

If the Office Assistant isn't visible, click the icon.

4. Click the **Options** button and explore the options. You may wish to change items to customize this feature to meet your needs.

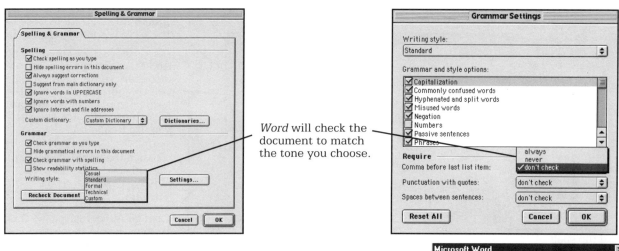

Word will check the document to match the tone you choose.

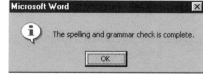

5. Press [ENTER] (Windows) [RETURN] (Macintosh) or click **OK** when the window tells you it is finished.

Human Brain
Not Yet Obsolete

Eye halve a spelling chequer,

It came with my pea sea.

It plainly marques four my revue

Miss steaks eye kin knot sea.

Eye strike a key and type a word,

And weight four it two say

Whether eye am wrong oar write;

It shows me strait a weigh.

As soon as a mist ache is maid,

It nose bee fore two long,

And eye can put the error rite;

Its rare lea ever wrong.

Eye have run this poem threw it.

Author Unknown

*As you can see, relying on spelling and grammar
checkers, and not proofreading, will cause problems!*

Use the Thesaurus

Learn to Use the Thesaurus

Word has a built-in thesaurus that is easy to access and easy to use!

> ### This Activity Covers the Following Topics
> * Replacing a Word
> * Looking Up a Word Within the Thesaurus

Replacing a Word

1. Open the file "Common Nouns" from the CD-ROM that came with this book.

2. **Double-click** the word "**house.**"

3. Choose **Language,** then **Thesaurus** from the **Tools** menu (Windows users can also press **SHIFT**F7; Macintosh users can also press ⌃⌘ **OPTION R**).

4. A list of meanings for the word "**house**" appears on the left side. Both nouns (n.) and verbs (v.) are shown. Synonyms for the word are on the right. Click the word "**home**" on the left side. New synonyms appear on the right side.

5. Click "**residence**" in the right column. Click **Replace,** and "**residence**" appears in the document.

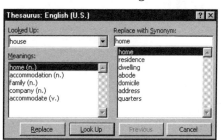 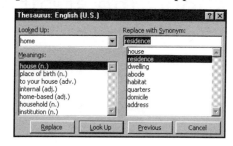

Looking Up a Word Within the Thesaurus

1. **Double-click** the word "**sack.**"

2. Choose **Language,** then **Thesaurus** from the **Tools** menu (Windows users can also press **SHIFT**F7; Macintosh users can also press ⌃⌘ **OPTION R**).

3. A list of meanings are on the left side. Synonyms for "sack" are on the right with the word "bag" selected.

4. Click **Look Up** to find synonyms for the word "**bag.**"

5. Click "**shopping bag**" in the list on the right. Click **Replace.**

 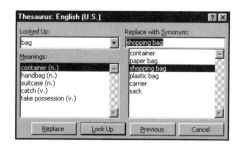

Customize *Word*

Make *Word* Easier for Beginners

Word has many unique features that make it one of the best-known word processing programs in the world. It is a very visual program, many formatting and editing features are available as buttons as well as in the menus. *Word* also provides intuitive help. For example, as you type, *Word* marks unknown words and grammatical errors with wavy lines. It also corrects common typos, and repeats paragraph formatting, e.g., if you type "teh," *Word* will change it to "the." If you begin a paragraph with a number, e.g., 1., in the next paragraph *Word* will type the "2." and indent as you did in the previous paragraph. Sometimes this help can be overwhelming for the new user. *Microsoft* allows you to customize *Word* to meet your needs. Don't worry, anything you change can be turned back on! In this activity you'll add frequently used buttons, create a button bar for primary-level students, try some of these unique text features and then turn them off and on.

This Activity Covers the Following Topics
- Changing the Toolbars
- Removing Buttons
- Creating a New Toolbar for Primary Students
- Viewing Only the Primary Students Toolbar
- Turning Off Automatic Spelling & Grammar Checking
- Using AutoCorrect
- Adding an AutoCorrect Entr
- Using AutoFormat
- Apply As You Type
- Ordinals with Superscript
- Changing the Quotes
- Changing the Default to 1" Margins

Changing the Toolbars

As you use *Word*, you'll find that there are certain activities that you do over and over. You can perform some of these activities more quickly if you can click them in the Standard, Formatting, or Drawing toolbars (these toolbars are usually visible on the screen). It is easy to add frequently used buttons to the toolbar.

1. Choose **Toolbars,** then **Customize** from the **View** menu.

2. Click the **Commands** tab.

3. Click **Insert** from **Categories.**

4. Scroll down in the **Commands** section until you find the **Clip Art** command.

5. Drag the **Clip Art** icon up to the **Standard** toolbar.

6. Adding other frequently used buttons, like **Format Picture** and **Insert Date,** may be helpful.

7. Adding frequently used Formatting commands can also make using *Word* faster. Click **Format** from **Categories.**

8. Drag **Change Case, Double-Space, and Drop Cap** into the Formatting toolbar. Click **Close.**

9. Click the **Change Case** button to see how it works.

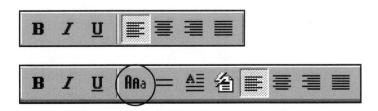

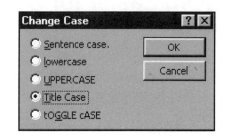

Removing Buttons

If there are buttons that you never use, you may wish to remove them to simplify the toolbar. Don't worry, any standard buttons you remove can be added again later.

1. Click the **Decrease Indent** button.

2. Press ALT (Windows) ⌘ (Macintosh) and drag the button down from the toolbar.

3. Add the button back to the button bar following the steps in the section above.

Creating a New Toolbar for Primary Students

The toolbar may be the easiest way for beginners and students in primary grades to manipulate *Word.* The standard toolbar contains so many buttons that it may be confusing.

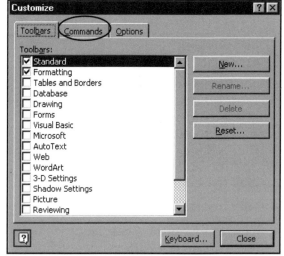

1. Choose **Customize** from the **Tools** menu.

2. Click **New.**

3. Name the new toolbar **Primary Grades.**

4. Leave **Normal** in the **Make toolbar available to:** section so everybody has access to the toolbar.

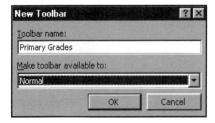

5. Click **OK.** A new toolbar appears.

6. Click the **Commands** tab.

7. Drag only the buttons beginners will use onto the toolbar. It grows as you add buttons. Click **Close** when you're finished.

Viewing Only the Primary Students Toolbar

1. Choose **Toolbars** from the **View** menu.

2. Remove the checks from all toolbars except **Primary Students**.

3. Click the blue title bar (striped in Macintosh) and drag the title bar into the proper place above the document if necessary. **Note:** This simplified toolbar can be modified at any time.

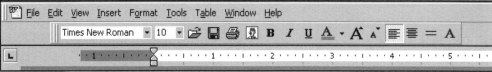

Creating toolbars specific to your students' abilities will save time and frustration for both the students and yourself.

Turning Off Automatic Spelling and Grammar Checking

1. Open the file "Spell Check Assign." Because it has so many errors, the paragraph is filled with red and green wavy lines. Documents you type may look like this, too. If you find the red and green wavy underlines distracting, you can turn them off and check the spelling and grammar at your convenience.

2. Choose **Option** (Preferences in *Word* 98) from the **Tools** menu.

3. Click the **Spelling & Grammar** tab.

4. Click the box next to **Check spelling as you type** to remove the check mark and click **OK**.

5. Type a **misspelled word** and press the Spacebar. No wavy red line should appear. You can still check the spelling when you want to.

6. Choose **Option** (Preferences in *Word* 98) from the **Tools** menu.

7. Click the **Spelling & Grammar** tab.

8. Click the box next to **Check grammar as you type** to deselect the feature and click **OK**. No wavy green line should appear when you make a grammatical error.

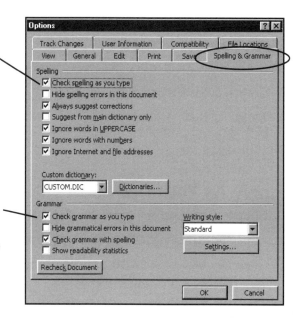

These options will remain turned off until you turn them back on. This action will affect every document you create, not just this document.

Using AutoCorrect

The AutoCorrect feature in *Word* will automatically detect and correct spelling, typographical, grammar, and capitalization errors. For example, if you type "studnet," and press the Spacebar, AutoCorrect replaces your word with "student."

1. Create a new *Word* document.

2. Type "**tthe**." While looking at the screen, press the Spacebar. "The" appears because "tthe" is one of the common typos entered into the AutoCorrect feature. The word is capitalized because **Capitalize first letter of sentence** is a default in **AutoCorrect**.

3. Type "**DOg.**" Again, look at the screen and press the Spacebar. "Dog" appears.

Adding an AutoCorrect Entry

1. By adding to the AutoCorrect list, you can make *Word* type frequently used words for you, for example, the name of your school. Choose **AutoCorrect** from the **Tools** menu.

2. Type "**jj**" in the **Replace** box.

3. Type "**Jefferson High School**" in the **With** box.

4. Click **Add** then **OK**.

5. Type "**jj.**" While looking at the screen, press the Spacebar. "Jefferson High School" appears.

Using AutoFormat

The AutoFormat feature in *Word* "memorizes" formatting in a paragraph and repeats it in the next.

1. Create a new *Word* document.

2. Type "**1. Red**" and press ⏎ENTER (Windows) ⏎RETURN (Macintosh). "2." appears because AutoFormat copies the format you defined in the previous line.

Apply As You Type

1. Choose **AutoCorrect** from the **Tools** menu.

2. Click the **AutoFormat As You Type** tab.

3. Click the box next to **Automatic numbered lists** to remove the check mark. Click **OK**.

4. Type "**1. Red**" and press ⏎ENTER (Windows) ⏎RETURN (Macintosh). The number "2" will not appear because you removed the check mark from Automatic numbered lists.

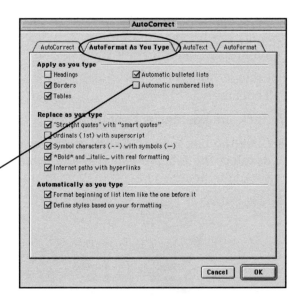

Ordinals with Superscript

Word automatically corrects a number of things when you type. This is usually helpful, but if you don't like it, you can turn off these defaults in the AutoCorrect menu. Here is an example that shows you how.

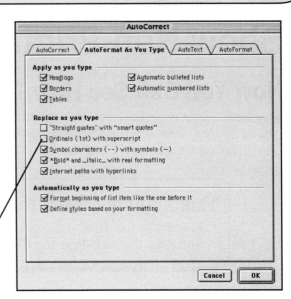

1. Create a new *Word* document.

2. Type "**1st**" and press ⌨ENTER (Windows) ⌨RETURN (Macintosh). The "st" changes to superscript.

3. Choose **AutoCorrect** from the **Tools** menu.

4. Click the **AutoFormat As You Type** tab.

5. Click the box next to **Ordinals (1st) with superscript** to remove the check mark.

6. Click **OK**.

7. Type "**1st**" again to see the difference.

Changing the Quotes

Most people prefer "smart quotes" in their documents. However, *Word* allows you to choose "straight quotes" if you wish.

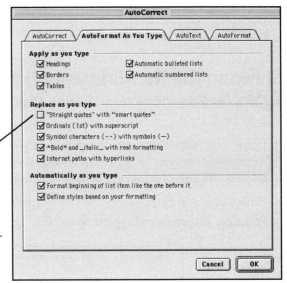

1. Type **"Quote"** (type the " " marks, too).

2. Choose **AutoCorrect** from the **Tools** menu.

3. Click the **AutoFormat As You Type** tab.

4. Click the box next to **"Straight quotes" with "smart quotes"** to remove the check mark.

5. Click **OK**.

6. Type **"Quote"** again. The quote marks will be straight.

7. Explore other changes you can make in AutoCorrect.

Changing the Default to 1" Margins

Most word processors have 1" margins as a default. *Word* has 1.25" left and right margins. If you prefer the standard 1" margins, you can change the default so a new document has 1" margins.

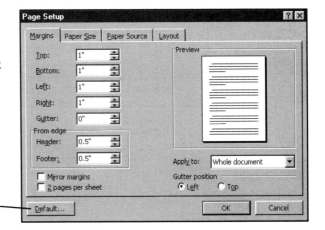

1. Choose **Page Setup** from the **File** menu (98 users choose **Document** from the **Format** menu).

2. Type "**1"**" margins in the **Left** and **Right** margin boxes.

3. Click the **Default** button.

   All new documents will have 1" margins.

Show Non-Printing Characters

Now You Can See How Things Happen

Microsoft *Word* will show you not only every letter you pressed while typing, it will also show you where you pressed the Spacebar, Tab key, and Return key. This is called "Showing the Non-Printing Characters." You activate this feature by using the mouse or key commands.

> ### This Activity Covers the Following Topics
> * Preparing the Text
> * Showing the Non-Printing Characters

Preparing the Text

1. Open the file "Field Trip Letter" from the CD-ROM that came with this book. The activity on page 25 uses this file to teach users to edit a *Word* file.

2. Complete the **Setting Tabs** section of the activity before you move on.

Showing the Non-Printing Characters

1. Click the **Show/Hide Non-Printing Characters** button ¶.

2. Using the **Non-Printing Character Key** on the right, interpret the text to see which keys were pressed. Notice the tab characters where you inserted tabs.

3. When you are finished, click the **Show/Hide Non-Printing Characters** button ¶ to hide the characters.

> ### Non-Printing Character Key
> →   Tab key was pressed
> •   Spacebar was pressed
> ¶   Enter/Return was pressed

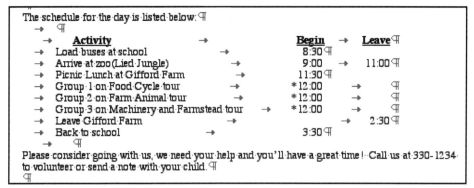

```
The·schedule·for·the·day·is·listed·below:¶
    →     ¶
        →    Activity              →              Begin  →   Leave¶
    →   Load·buses·at·school            →         8:30¶
    →   Arrive·at·zoo(Lied·Jungle)         →      9:00   →  11:00¶
    →   Picnic·Lunch·at·Gifford·Farm       →      11:30¶
    →   Group·1·on·Food·Cycle·tour         →      *12:00  →       ¶
    →   Group·2·on·Farm·Animal·tour        →      *12:00  →       ¶
    →   Group·3·on·Machinery·and·Farmstead·tour  → *12:00 →      ¶
    →   Leave·Gifford·Farm                          →  2:30¶
    →   Back·to·school           →          3:30¶
    →     ¶
Please·consider·going·with·us,·we·need·your·help·and·you'll·have·a·great·time!·Call·us·at·330-1234·
to·volunteer·or·send·a·note·with·your·child.¶
¶
```

When students ask for help with a Word *document, click the **Show/Hide Non-Printing Characters** button to see which keys they have pressed. This solves the* ¶ *mysterious "I never touched a key and look what it did!" dilemma.*

Change the Case of Text

Make *Word* Correct Your Capitalization Errors

Have you ever been typing along, then stopped to look at the monitor only to find that you had the Caps Lock key down and everything was capitalized? Or have you ever told a student, "I'm sorry, you'll have to type the whole thing over again because it's all caps!"? *Word* makes it easy to change the case of text.

> ### This Activity Covers the Following Topics
> - Changing Text from Caps to Sentence Case
> - Changing Text from Sentence Case to Title Case
> - Changing Text from Title Case to tOGGLE cASE

Changing Text from Caps to Sentence Case

1. Create a new *Word* document.

2. Press [CAPS LOCK]. Type the following text: "**DON'T YOU HATE IT WHEN YOU TYPE A WHOLE PARAGRAPH AND THEN DISCOVER THE CAPS LOCK KEY WAS PRESSED?**"

3. Select the text.

4. Choose **Change Case** from the **Format** menu.

5. Choose **Sentence Case**. Click **OK**.

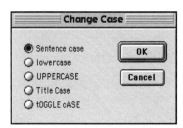

> Don't you hate it when you type a whole paragraph and then discover the caps lock key was pressed?

Changing Text from Sentence Case to Title Case

1. Choose **Change Case** from the **Format** menu.

2. Choose **Title Case**. Click **OK**.

> Don't You Hate It When You Type A Whole Paragraph And Then Discover The Caps Lock Key Was Pressed?

Changing Text from Title Case to tOGGLE cASE

1. Choose **Change Case** from the **Format** menu.

2. Choose **tOGGLE cASE**. Click **OK**.

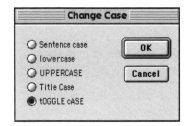

> dON'T yOU hATE iT wHEN yOU tYPE a wHOLE pARAGRAPH aND tHEN dISCOVER tHE cAPS lOCK kEY wAS pRESSED?

3. Choose **Change Case** from the **Format** menu.

4. Choose **lowercase.** Click **OK**.

5. Choose **Change Case** from the **Format** menu.

6. Choose **UPPERCASE.** Click **OK**.

Use Comments

Use Comments to Give Feedback on Papers

Instead of handwriting feedback on student papers, use the Comments function of *Word* to type it. Students will love getting electronic feedback!

This Activity Covers the Following Topics
- Inserting Comments
- Editing the Document
- Viewing the Comments
- Deleting a Comment

Inserting Comments

1. Open the file "Writing Assignment" from the CD-ROM that came with this book.

2. Click anywhere within the word "**good**" in the second paragraph.

3. Choose **Comment** from the **Insert** menu.

4. The comments dialog box appears on the screen. The cursor is blinking in the **Comments From** box. Type "**The word "well" is the correct choice.**"

5. Click **Close**. The word "good" is highlighted in yellow to indicate a comment has been inserted.

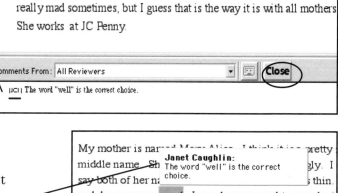

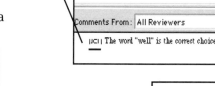

6. Move the cursor over the word "good" without clicking the mouse button. The comment you inserted will appear.

7. Click on the word "**not**" in the third paragraph. This is a really long sentence that needs to be fixed.

8. Choose **Comment** from the **Insert** menu. Type this comment: "**Try improving this sentence. Read it out loud and see if it is easy to read. Making it into two sentences may be a good idea.**" Click **Close**.

9. Click on the last word in the fourth paragraph. Choose **Comment** from the **Insert** menu. Type this comment: "**Read this paragraph out loud. You'll notice that almost every sentence begins with the word "She". See what you can do to add variety. Target is a name so it needs a capital letter.**" Click **Close**.

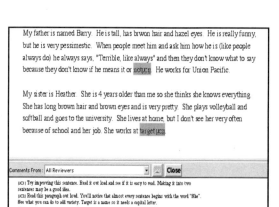

Editing the Document

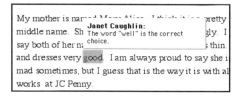

1. Now you're going to be the student and make the edits. Move your cursor over the highlighted word to see the comment.

2. Click to the left of the word and type the suggested word "**well**." Both "well" and "good" are on the line. Sometimes it helps students to keep the comment until the changes are made in case they need to refer to it again.

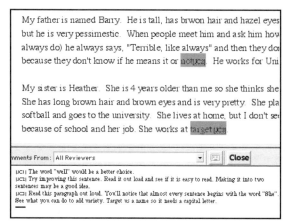

3. Click between the word "**good**" and the **period**. Press the **Backspace** key (Macintosh users press the **Delete** key) to delete the comment and the original word.

Viewing the Comments

1. There is another way to view comments. All of the comments will show in this method. Choose **Comment** from the **View** menu.

2. Read the **second comment** and **fix the sentence**.

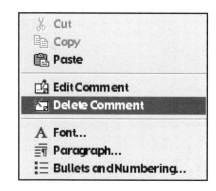

Deleting a Comment

Now that you've fixed the sentence, you no longer need the comment, but you don't want to delete the selected word.

1. Right-click the comment (Macintosh users [CTRL]-click).

2. Choose **Delete Comment**. The comment and the highlighting will be removed.

Students will be eager to do Peer Editing if they can use the Comments function in Word to do it!

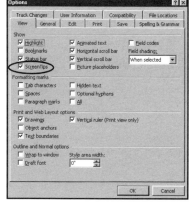

If the comments don't show when you move your cursor over the word, choose Options (Preferences in earlier versions) from the Tools menu. Click the View tab, then Screen Tips.

Format Painter

Jazz Up a Worksheet

Formatting a document can be very time-consuming, especially if you make several changes to enhance the text. Using Format Painter can make this task incredibly easy and fun. This activity will show you how fun and easy formatting can be.

> **This Activity Covers the Following Topics**
> - Formatting the Text
> - Using Format Painter

Formatting the Text

1. Open the file "American Artists" from the CD-ROM that came with this book.

2. Select the name "**John James Audubon.**"

3. Choose **Font** from the **Format** menu.

4. Choose **Bold** from **Font style**, **16** from **Size**, and **Small caps** from **Effects**. Click **OK**.

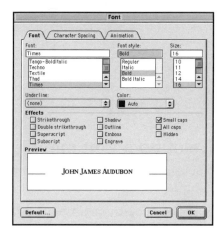

Using Format Painter

1. With the name John James Audubon selected, double-click the **Format Painter** icon.

2. Click "**John**" in John Singleton Copley. The word is formatted like the previous artist.

3. Select **Singleton Copley**. The words have the same format.

4. Format the rest of the artists' names using **Format Painter**.

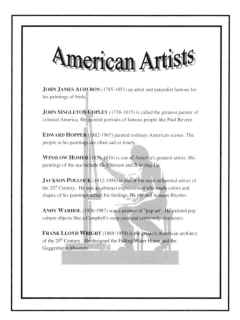

Set Tabs

Learn to Create a Schedule

Tabs can be frustrating until you learn to use them. Different tabs allow you to move text in different ways. This lesson will show you how they work.

> ### This Activity Covers the Following Topic
> • Setting Tabs

Setting Tabs

1. Open the file "Setting Tabs" from the CD-ROM that came with this book.

2. **Highlight the text** under the heading **"Different Types of Tabs & What They Do."**

3. Click the **1/2"** mark on the ruler. A left tab will be inserted.

4. Click the **Tab Box** two times to choose a center tab.

5. Click on the ruler's **2"** mark to insert the **Center** tab.

6. Click a Right tab under the **3 1/2"** mark on the ruler.

7. Click a Decimal tab under the **4 1/2"** mark on the ruler.

Left Tab
Center Tab
Right Tab
Decimal Tab

Different Types of Tabs & What They Do			
left	center	right	1.2345
lef	center	righ	12.345
le	center	rig	123.45
l	center	ri	1234.5
left	center	r	12345
lef	center	right	12345
le	cent	righ	1234
l	cen	rig	123
left	ce	ri	12
lef	c	r	1

When typing new documents, text won't move just because you set tabs in the ruler. You need to press the Tab key inside the text to move it. In this lesson, the text moved because tabs were put into the document when it was originally typed by pressing the Tab key in front of each section. The tab icons were then removed from the ruler. This allowed you to immediately see how different types of tabs change text location after you inserted the new tabs.

Notice how the text is aligned under each tab marker. The text under the Left tab is aligned on the left side. The text under the Center tab is centered under the tab. The text under the Right tab is aligned on the right side. The text under the Decimal tab is aligned on the decimal point.

8. Scroll down until the word **"Schedule"** is the top line on the screen. **Highlight the text under** the title **"Schedule."**

9. Click a **Right** tab at **1 1/2"**, a **Left tab** at **2"**, and a **Decimal** tab at **4"**.

Schedule		
8:15	Nebraska History	20
9:09	American History	17
10:07	American History	19
11:00	Lunch	100
11:27	Nebraska History	17
12:24	Plan	
1:16	Geography	16
2:05	Geography	15

To remove a tab, click and drag the tab marker below the ruler and release the mouse.

Indent Text

Make a List That Wraps

You can tell *Word* to indent text for you. It will save you time and make your documents look great! It's so easy!

This Activity Covers the Following Topics
- Indenting the First Line
- Creating a Hanging Indent

Indenting the First Line

1. Create a **new** *Word* document.

2. Drag the **top triangle** (First Line Indent marker) of the left margin marker to the .5" mark on the ruler.

3. Type the **text in the screen shot below**. Read it as you type to learn about this technique.

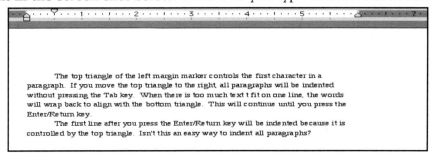

The top triangle of the left margin marker controls the first character in a paragraph. If you move the top triangle to the right, all paragraphs will be indented without pressing the Tab key. When there is too much text t fit on one line, the words will wrap back to align with the bottom triangle. This will continue until you press the Enter/Return key.

The first line after you press the Enter/Return key will be indented because it is controlled by the top triangle. Isn't this an easy way to indent all paragraphs?

Creating a Hanging Indent

1. Create a **new** *Word* document.

2. Drag the **bottom triangle** (Hanging Indent marker) of the left margin marker **one ruler mark to the right**. **Hint**: Place the cursor arrow on the triangle, not the rectangle.

3. Type "**1.**" Press [TAB], then type the rest of the **text in the screen shot below** for point number 1. Do not press [ENTER] (Windows) [RETURN] (Macintosh) until the end of the sentence because it will cause the next line to return to the left margin.

4. **Type** the rest of the **text**.

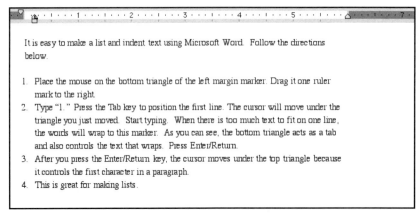

It is easy to make a list and indent text using Microsoft Word. Follow the directions below.

1. Place the mouse on the bottom triangle of the left margin marker. Drag it one ruler mark to the right.
2. Type "1." Press the Tab key to position the first line. The cursor will move under the triangle you just moved. Start typing. When there is too much text to fit on one line, the words will wrap to this marker. As you can see, the bottom triangle acts as a tab and also controls the text that wraps. Press Enter/Return.
3. After you press the Enter/Return key, the cursor moves under the top triangle because it controls the first character in a paragraph.
4. This is great for making lists.

Leader Tabs

Create a Short Answer Test

Leader tabs draw a line from text to a tab location. For example, in tables of contents they are used to draw a dotted line from the title of the section to the page number. This activity will help you make a checklist and a form, using leader tabs to draw the lines.

> ### This Activity Covers the Following Topics
> * Preparing *Word* for This Activity
> * Changing Apply As You Type
> * Creating Leader Tabs
> * Using Leader Tabs
> * Creating a Form Using Leader Tabs

Preparing *Word* for This Activity

Word has some helpful options including AutoFormat. However, occasionally you need to turn them off to create a document. In this activity you will learn how to create a "short answer" test with "answer" lines. In order to make *Word* draw the lines, you must modify the AutoFormat options.

Changing Apply As You Type

1. Create a new *Word* document.

2. Choose **AutoCorrect** from the **Tools** menu.

3. Click the **AutoFormat As You Type** tab.

4. Click the box next to **Automatic numbered lists** to remove the check mark.

5. Click **OK**.

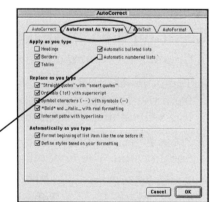

Creating Leader Tabs

1. Click the **Tab Box** three times to choose a **Decimal** tab.

2. Click the **1"** mark on the ruler to insert the **Decimal** tab.

3. Drag the **bottom triangle** (Hanging Indent marker) of the left margin marker to the **1 1/4"** mark.

4. Choose **Tabs** from the **Format** menu.

5. Click the **radio button** next to "**4** ____" in the Leader section of the box. This choice will draw a line when you press the ⌨TAB key.

6. Click **Set**, then **OK**.

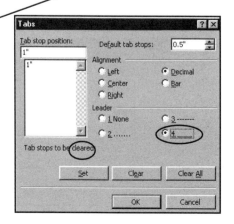

Using Leader Tabs

1. Press ⟦TAB⟧. A line (leader) is drawn (see the screen shot below).

2. Press the Spacebar twice.

3. Type "**9.**"

4. Type "**A leader tab will draw a line to the left of the tab position when the Tab key is pressed**."

5. Press ⟦ENTER⟧ (Windows) ⟦RETURN⟧ (Macintosh) twice.

6. Press ⟦TAB⟧. A line (leader) is drawn.

7. Press the Spacebar.

8. Type "**10.**" **Note**: You only press the Spacebar twice if you are typing a single-digit number. The spaces take the place of the first digit. If you don't press the Spacebar, the lines for single-digit numbers will be longer than those for double-digit numbers.

9. Type the text in the screen shot below.

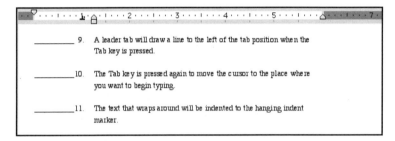

Creating a Form Using Leader Tabs

1. Create a new *Word* document.

2. Type the word "**Name.**" Click a **Left** tab just to the left of the right margin marker. Choose **Tabs** from the **Format** menu. Click the radio button next to "**4** ____." Click **Set**, then **OK**. Press ⟦TAB⟧. A line will be drawn from the space to the tab marker.

3. Press ⟦ENTER⟧ (Windows) ⟦RETURN⟧ (Macintosh) twice. Type the word "**Address.**" **Press** ⟦TAB⟧ to draw another line. The line will go to the end because you inserted that tab in step 2.

4. Press ⟦ENTER⟧ (Windows) ⟦RETURN⟧ (Macintosh) twice. Type the word "**City.**" Click a **Left** tab on the **4 1/2"** mark. Choose **Tab** from the **Format** menu. **Select** the 4 1/2" tab. **Click** in the **solid line** radio button. Click **Set**, then **OK**. Press ⟦TAB⟧. A line will be drawn.

5. **Type** the word "**State.**" Click a **Right** tab on the **5 3/4"** mark. Choose **Tab** from the **Format** menu. **Select** the 5 3/4" tab. Click in the **solid line** radio button. Click **Set**, then **OK**. Press ⟦TAB⟧ to draw a line. **Type** the word "**Zip.**" **Press the Spacebar**. Press ⟦TAB⟧ to draw a line. The line will go to the end because you inserted that tab in step 2.

6. Good job! Press ⟦CTRL⟧⟦S⟧ (Windows) ⟦⌘⟧⟦S⟧ (Macintosh) or choose **Save** from the **File** menu to save your file.

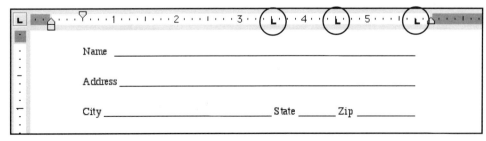

Page Numbers, Headers/Footers

Put Automatic Page Numbers in a Document

You can automatically insert information such as the page number, title, and date on every page in a header or footer. A *header* appears at the top of every printed page in a document. A *footer* appears at the bottom of every page. This will save you time and give your document a finished, professional appearance. This activity will show you how it all works.

This Activity Covers the Following Topics

- Inserting Automatic Page Numbers
- Inserting a Page Break
- Inserting a Header
- Inserting a Fixed Date
- Inserting a Changing Date

Inserting Automatic Page Numbers

You can insert automatic page numbers anywhere in a document, but they usually appear in a header or footer.

1. Open the file "Field Trip Letter" from the CD-ROM that came with this book. The activity on page 25 uses this file to teach users to edit a *Word* file. You may complete that activity first, or use this file as it is.

2. Choose **Header and Footer** from the **View** menu. A rectangle drawn with dashes appears at the top of the page to indicate the header location. The Header and Footer toolbar appears.

3. Click the **Switch Between Header and Footer** button on the toolbar 🔁. The rectangle moves to the bottom of the page.

4. Click the **Page Number** button on the toolbar 🔢. The number is left justified.

5. Click 🔲 or ≡ to center the number.

6. To add the word "Page" before the number, click to the left of the number, type the word "**Page**," and add a **space**.

7. Click **Insert AutoText** to view automatic options. If you choose them, you may need to delete previously inserted text.

8. Click the **Close** button to see the document.

The footer appears in a light gray color but it will print normally.

Inserting a Page Break

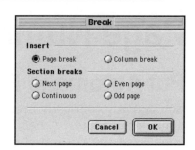

1. You can decide where you want a new page to be created in a document. **Click at the beginning of the first paragraph.** You're going to insert a page break.

2. Choose **Break** from the **Insert** menu. The Break dialog box appears with Page Break selected.

3. Click **OK.** The text after the cursor has moved to a new page.

4. **Scroll down** to check out the footers. Remember, they will be printed in a light gray color.

Inserting a Header

1. Choose **Header and Footer** from the **View** menu.

2. Type **your name** in the header, then click **Close.** Your name will appear at the top of each page in a light gray color.

Inserting a Fixed Date

1. Select the date at the top of the page.

2. Choose **Date and Time** from the **Insert** menu. Click **OK.** Today's date appears in the place of the previous date.

Inserting a Changing Date

Do you send out the same field trip announcements or letters every year? If you insert a changing date into the document, the current date will appear every time you open it. That way you won't have to manually change it. There are two ways to insert a changing date.

1. Choose **Date and Time** from the **Insert** menu. Click to insert a check mark in **Update Automatically.** Click **OK.** The date will look the same, but it will always show the date that you open the file.

2. **Delete** the **date** at the top of the letter.

3. Choose **Field** from the **Insert** menu.

4. Click **Date and Time** in the **left box, then Date in the right box.**

5. Click the **Options** button.

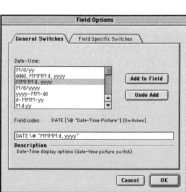

The first method is much faster!

6. Click **MMMM d, yyyy,** then **Add to Field.** Click **OK.**

7. Click **OK** again. The date is inserted in the document. Every time you open this document the current date will appear.

Create a Math Worksheet

Make a Fractions Worksheet for Your Class

Word has a built-in equation editor so you can make professional-looking math worksheets. Follow these directions to make a fractions worksheet.

> ### This Activity Covers the Following Topics
> - Creating a Math Worksheet
> - Creating an Equation
> - Editing the Equation

Creating a Math Worksheet

1. Create a new *Word* document.

2. Choose **24 Point** from the **Size Box** in the Formatting toolbar `24 ▾`.

3. Click the **Center** button `≡`.

4. Click the **Bold** button `B` or press `CTRL``B` (Windows) `⌘``B` (Macintosh).

5. **Type** "Simplify:" and **press** `ENTER` (Windows) `RETURN` (Macintosh) **twice**.

6. Click the **Align Left** button `≡`.

7. Click the **Bold** button `B` or press `CTRL``B` (Windows) `⌘``B` (Macintosh) to remove the boldfacing.

8. **Type** "1.". **Press** `TAB`. **Type** "3.".

Creating an Equation

1. Choose **Object** from the **Insert** menu.

2. Click **Microsoft Equation** and click **OK**. The Equation Editor toolbar appears.

3. Click the **second option from the left** in the **bottom row,** then choose the **first option on the left**.

4. Two boxes representing the number positions in a fraction appear. Type "**2,**" then press `TAB` to move the cursor down to the bottom box. Type "**4**" (*Word* 98 types the text inside the Equation Editor box).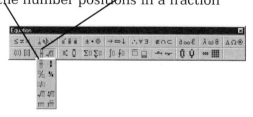

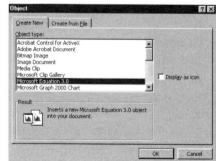

5. **Click outside the equation box** in the *Word* document (*Word* 98 users click the close box in the upper left corner).

Windows

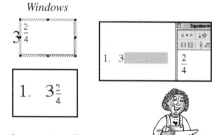

Microsoft Equation does not install automatically. You'll need to do a custom install.

Editing the Equation

Double-click the **fraction**. The Equation Editor appears. Change the fraction.

Draw a Border

Make a Classroom Rules Poster

Borders can make simple text suitable for framing. They can also be used to emphasize text. *Word* provides many border options, allowing you to give your document just the right look.

This Activity Covers the Following Topics
- Preparing the Text
- Indenting the List
- Adding a Title Border
- Shading the Title
- Adding a Page Border
- Removing a Page Border
- Inserting a Graphic Border
- Creating an AutoShapes Border
- Editing the AutoShape

Preparing the Text

1. Open the file "Golden Rule" from the CD-ROM that came with this book. This file contains some "good sense" rules for cooperation. You're going to jazz it up to post it in your classroom.

2. It is easier to add borders if you can see the entire document. Click the arrow on the **Zoom Box** on the **Standard toolbar** and choose **50%** `50%` or choose **Zoom** from the **View** menu. The document is reduced to 50% so you can see the entire page.

3. Press `CTRL A` (Windows) `⌘ A` (Macintosh) or choose **Select All** from **Edit** to select the text.

4. Choose a font that seems exactly right for the message of the text by clicking the **Font Box** `Verdana` or choosing **Font** from the **Format** menu.

5. Choose **24** point from the Font Size box `24` or choose **Font** from the **Format** menu. **Note**: Fonts are not all the same size. If 24 point seems too large for your font or the text moves to another page, you may need to choose a smaller size.

6. Select the **title** only and make it **36** point.

7. Click the **Center** button `≡` or choose **Paragraph** from the **Format** menu, then choose **Center** from the alignment choices.

Indenting the List

1. **Select the text** under the title. The text on some lines wraps onto another line. It would look better if it was aligned under the first word of the rule.

2. Click a **Decimal tab** to align the numbers properly `[ruler]`. **Note**: More information about inserting Decimal tabs can be found on page 45.

3. Drag the **bottom triangle** of the **Left Margin marker** to the **right of the tab** to align the text `[ruler]`. **Note**: More information about using this hanging indent can be found on page 46.

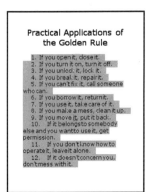

Adding a Title Border

1. **Select** the **title**.

2. Choose **Borders and Shading** from the **Format** menu.

3. Click the **Borders** tab.

4. Click **Shadow** under **Setting**.

5. Click **3 pt** from the **Width** menu.

6. Choose **Paragraph** from the **Apply to** menu.

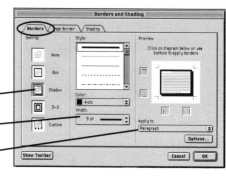

Shading the Title

1. Click the **Shading** tab.

2. Choose a **color** and click **OK**.

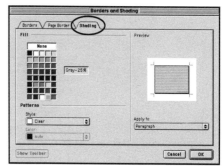

Try other options for borders. You can change the color, too.

Adding a Page Border

1. Choose **Borders and Shading** from the **Format** menu.

2. Click the **Page Border** tab.

3. Click **Box** under **Setting**.

4. Click **3 pt** from the **Width** menu.

5. Choose **Whole Document** from the **Apply to** menu.

6. Click **OK**.

7. **Print** the document.

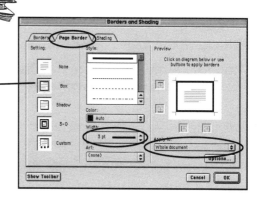

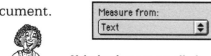

If the borders are cut off, choose Borders and Shading from the Format menu. Click the Page Border tab. Click Options. Choose Text in the "Measure from" menu. Click OK and print again.

Removing a Page Border

1. Choose **Borders and Shading** from the **Format** menu.

2. Click the **Page Border** tab.

3. Click **None** under **Setting**.

4. Click **OK**. The outside border is removed.

5. Choose **Borders and Shading** from the **Format** menu.

6. Click the **Borders** tab.

7. Click **None** under **Setting**.

8. Click **OK**. The title border is removed.

Practical Applications of
the Golden Rule

1. If you open it, close it.
2. If you turn it on, turn it off.
3. If you unlock it, lock it.
4. If you break it, repair it.
5. If you can't fix it, call someone who can.
6. If you borrow it, return it.
7. If you use it, take care of it.
8. If you make a mess, clean it up.
9. If you move it, put it back.
10. If it belongs to somebody else and you want to use it, get permission.
11. If you don't know how to operate it, leave it alone.
12. If it doesn't concern you, don't mess with it.

Inserting a Graphic Border

1. Choose **Borders and Shading** from the **Format** menu.

2. Click the **Page Border** tab.

3. Click **Box** under **Setting**.

4. Click the menu under **Art** and choose a border.

5. Click **OK**.

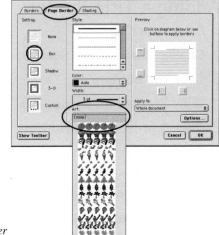

If the toolbar isn't showing, click the View menu, choose Toolbars, and then WordArt.

You don't have to border all sides. Click the Border boxes to see what they do.

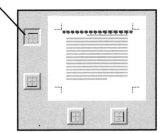

Creating an AutoShapes Border

1. **Remove the page border** (turn to page 53 for help).

2. Choose **AutoShapes** from the **Drawing** toolbar, or choose **Picture**, then **AutoShapes** from the **Insert** menu.

3. Choose **Basic Shapes** and **drag to the right** until the palette tears off and stays on the screen.

4. Click the **Rounded Rectangle** shape.

5. Place the **+** shaped cursor on the upper left corner of the page. **Click and drag** to draw a rectangle around the text. The shape will cover the text, but you'll fix that next.

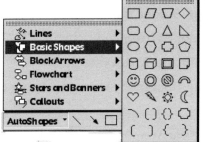

Editing the AutoShape

1. Choose **No Fill** from the **Fill Color icon** on the Drawing toolbar. The text will appear because the rounded rectangle is now transparent.

2. Choose **More Lines** from the **Line Style icon** ≡.

3. Type "**16**" in the **Weight** box. Click **OK**.

4. Click the arrow next to the **Line Color icon** .

5. Choose **Patterned Lines**.

6. Choose a **pattern**. Click **OK**.

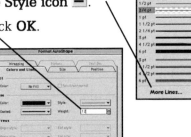

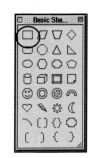

Bulleted Lists

Create Supplies Checklists

Do you have trouble getting parents and students to follow through on supplies lists you send home? Give them a list with boxes and they automatically start checking it off. In this activity you'll learn how to make all of your lists into checklists!

This Activity Covers the Following Topics
- Adding Bullets to a List
- Adding Bullets to Part of a Document
- Sorting the Text
- Changing the Case of the Text
- Adding Bullets to the List

Adding Bullets to a List

1. Open the file "School Supplies" from the CD-ROM that came with this book.

2. **Select** (highlight) the **list**.

3. Choose **Bullets and Numbering** from the **Format** menu.

4. Click the **Bulleted** tab.

5. Choose the **Checkbox list**.

6. Click the **Customize** button.

7. Click the **Font** button.

8. Choose **22** from the **Font Size** choices. Click **OK,** then **OK** again.

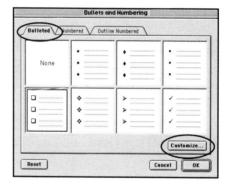

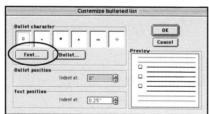

Larger boxes are more inviting to the user!

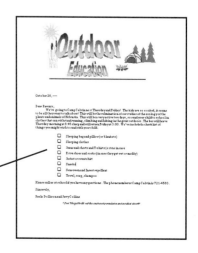

Adding Bullets to Part of a Document

1. Open the file "Outdoor Ed Letter" from the CD-ROM that came with this book.

2. **Select** (highlight) the **list of supplies in the middle of the letter**.

3. Drag the **Left Margin** marker to 1" on the ruler.

4. Following the directions above, **make this into a checklist**.

Sorting the Text

1. Open the file "Classroom Inventory" from the CD-ROM that came with this book.

2. **Select** (highlight) the **list**.

3. Choose **Sort** from the **Table** menu.

4. Click **OK**. The list is alphabetized.

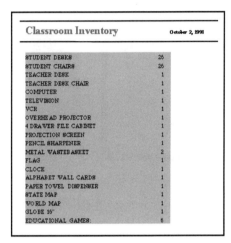
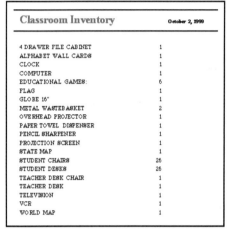

Changing the Case of the Text

This list would look better if it wasn't typed in all capital letters.

1. **Select** (highlight) the **list**.

2. Choose **Change Case** from the **Format** menu.

3. Choose **Title Case** and click **OK**.

Adding Bullets to the List

1. Click the **Bullet** button ⊞ .

2. Choose **Bullets and Numbering** from the **Format** menu.

3. **Choose a format** then click **OK**.

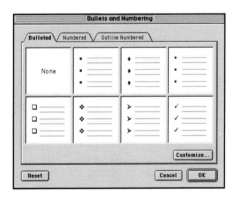

Click the Customize button, then the Bullet button to see the great bullets you can create.

Section Breaks

Insert an Outline in Part of a Document

Have you ever wanted to put columns in just part of a document? Inserting a section break allows you to do this. Section breaks are also used to create different headers and footers, page numbers, and to vary the number of columns in sections of a document.

> ### This Activity Covers the Following Topics
> - Learning About the Document
> - Inserting a Section Break
> - Inserting a Column Break

Learning About the Document

This letter informing parents of an upcoming assignment contains a list of items containing computer chips. It would take up less space if these items were in two columns.

1. Open the file "Computer Letter" from the CD-ROM that came with this book.

2. Click on the first item in the list, "**Video games**." Click the **Column button** and drag to select two columns. The entire document is in two columns, but only the list needs to be in columns. You can remedy this by inserting a section break.

3. Click the **Column button** again and reduce the columns to **one**.

Inserting a Section Break

1. Click to the **left** of the word "**Video**" in the list. Choose **Break** from the **Insert** menu.

2. Choose **Continuous** from the dialog box. This forces the new section to begin on this line. Click **OK**.

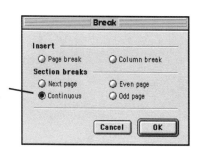

3. Click the **Column button** and drag to select **two columns**.

4. The closing paragraph is at the bottom of the second column. Click to the **left** of "**Your child...**" and **insert a section break**. Choose **Continuous**.

5. Click the **Column button** and select **one** column.

6. Press [ENTER] (Windows) [RETURN] (Macintosh) to insert a blank line between the columns section and the closing paragraph.

Inserting a Column Break

1. The first column has more text than the second. Click to the **left** of "**Sprinkler System**" at the bottom of the first column.

2. Choose **Break** from the **Insert** menu.

3. Choose **Column break** and click **OK**. This forces "Sprinkler System" to move to the second column.

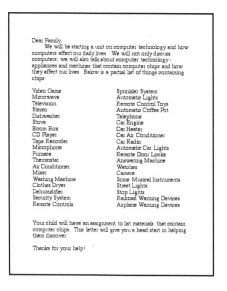

Decorative Characters

Give Your Text a Formal Look

This feature in the *Word* program puts text creativity at your fingertips. Letters and numbers can become graphic works of art that set the mood for quotes or stories.

> ### This Activity Covers the Following Topics
> - Creating a Raised Initial Cap
> - Creating a Dropped Initial Cap

Creating a Raised Initial Cap

A raised initial cap is used to create a mood in a document. It is characterized by a noticeably taller first letter.

1. Create a new *Word* document.

2. Type in the following quote from Albert Einstein: **"Great spirits have always encountered violent opposition."**

3. Click and drag to **select** the letter **"G."**

4. Choose **36** point from the **Font Size** box 36. 24 or 36 point works well for an initial cap when you have 12-point text. The text below is 12 point and the "G" is 36 point.

> Great spirits have always encountered violent opposition.

5. Try different fonts until you find one that suggests the mood of the quote.

Creating a Dropped Initial Cap

A dropped initial cap is just what the name implies. The first letter is dropped below the baseline.

1. Create a new *Word* document.

2. Type the following text: **"Love has been characterized by Einstein. He said, "Gravity cannot be held responsible for people falling in love".**"

3. **Select** the quote. Move the **Right Margin marker** to **1 3/4"** so the quote will run on five lines.

4. Choose **Drop Cap** from the **Format** menu.

5. Click **Dropped.** You can also change the Font if you wish.
   Click **OK**.

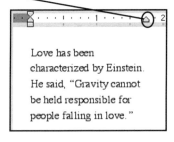

Learn About Graphics

Understand How Graphics Work

Graphics can add so much to a document. This activity will help you understand the wrap and insertion options available in *Word*.

> ### This Activity Covers the Following Topics
> - Inserting Clip Art
> - Wrapping Tight
> - Wrapping Square
> - Wrapping Top & Bottom
> - Wrapping None
> - Using Advanced Layout
> - Inserting Pictures into a Text Box

Inserting Clip Art

1. Open the file "Text" from the CD-ROM that came with this book.

2. Place the cursor at the beginning of the second paragraph and click.

3. Click the **Clip Art** icon or choose **Picture,** then **Clip Art** from the **Insert** menu. **Choose and insert a picture**.

4. **Drag** on a handle (one of the boxes surrounding the picture) **to resize** the picture.

Wrapping Tight

1. **Right-click** the picture (Macintosh users [CTRL] click). Choose **Format Picture.**

2. Click the **Layout** tab (Wrapping in *Word* 98 & *Word* 97).

3. Choose the **Tight** option and click **OK.**

4. **Move the picture** around and watch the text wrap around the picture.

Wrapping Square

1. **Right-click** the picture (Macintosh users [CTRL] click). Choose **Format Picture.**

2. Choose the **Layout** tab (Wrapping in *Word* 98 & *Word* 97).

3. Choose the **Square** option and click **OK.**

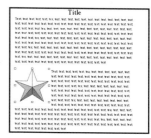

Wrapping Top & Bottom

1. Choose **Picture** from the **Format** menu.

2. Click the **Layout** tab (Wrapping in *Word* 98 & *Word* 97).

3. Click the **Top & Bottom** option and click **OK**.

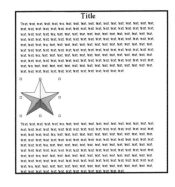

Wrapping None

1. Click the **Text Wrapping** icon on the **Picture** toolbar.

2. Choose the **None** option.

3. Click the **Text Wrapping** icon on

4. Choose the **Through** option.

If the toolbar isn't showing, click the View menu, choose Toolbars, and then Picture.

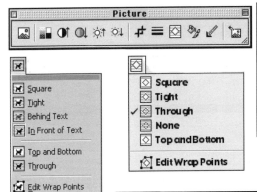

Using Advanced Layout   **2000 only**

1. Choose **Picture** from the **Format** menu.

2. Click the **Layout** tab.

3. Click the **Advanced** button. Try the **In front of text** and **In line with text** options.

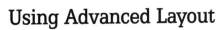

Inserting Pictures into a Text Box

Inserting pictures into a text box can give you additional flexibility.

1. **Draw a text box** in the middle of the first paragraph.

2. Using the directions from the previous page, insert **clip art into the box**.

3. Choose **Text Box** from the **Format** menu.

4. Choose **Tight** and click **OK**.

Insert a Picture from a File

Create a Graphic Study Guide

A picture is worth a thousand words. This is especially true when you're trying to teach a complicated topic. This activity will teach you to create a graphic worksheet for your students.

> ### This Activity Covers the Following Topics
> - Inserting a Picture from a File
> - Labeling the Picture
> - Creating Arrowhead Lines

Inserting a Picture from a File

1. Create a new *Word* document.

2. Choose **48** from the **Font Size box** [48 ▾].

3. Click the **Center** button ≣.

4. Type "**Parts of a Flower**."

5. Press [ENTER] (Windows) [RETURN] (Macintosh) **twice** to move the cursor down.

6. Choose **Picture,** then **From File** from the **Insert** menu. **Note:** *Word* 2000 users may wish to draw a large Text Box under the title, then insert the picture into the box. This allows greater flexibility in moving the picture. Text boxes are discussed in the next topic if you need help.

7. Navigate to the **Pictures** folder on the CD-ROM that came with this book. Double-click the **Lily** picture.

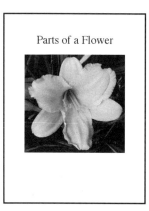

Parts of a Flower

Labeling the Picture

1. Click the **Text Box** icon from the **Drawing** toolbar 🖺 or choose **Text Box** from the **Insert** menu.

2. Hold the mouse button down and **drag to draw a text box below the picture on the left side**.

3. Choose **22** from the **Font Size** box.

4. Type "**Petal**" in the text box. [Petal]

5. The text box is outlined with a thin line. Choose **No Line** from the **Line Color icon** ✏▾.

6. Using this method create labels reading "**Stigma**" and "**Stamen**."

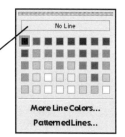

Parts of a Flower

Petal   Stigma   Stamen

Creating Arrowhead Lines

1. Click the **Arrow** tool ↖.

2. Hold [SHIFT] and drag to draw a line from the label "**Petal**" to a petal.

3. Click the **Line Style** icon ≣ and choose **2 1/4 pt.**

4. Click the **Line Color** icon ✏▾ and choose a contrasting color.

5. **Draw arrows** from the **other two labels** to their corresponding parts.

Insert a Movie

Create a Self-Study Sheet with a Movie

As teachers, we're always trying to find new ways to motivate students. Why not make a self-study sheet to teach students a concept? In this activity you'll make a study sheet about butterflies and pollination that includes a movie of a bee getting nectar from a sunflower. You won't believe how easy it is to add a movie to a document!

> ## This Activity Covers the Following Topics
> * Preparing the File
> * Inserting a Movie into a File
> * Playing the Movie
> * Saving the File

Preparing the File

1. Open the file "Butterfly" from the CD-ROM that came with this book.

   This file is a study sheet to teach students about butterflies. You're going to insert a movie into the space between the paragraphs.

2. **Place the cursor one line down** from the bottom of the first paragraph and click.

Inserting a Movie into a File   `2000 only`

3. Click the **Insert Clip Art icon** 📷 or choose **Picture**, then **Clip Art** from the **Insert** menu.

4. Click the **Movie Clips tab**.

5. Click **Import Clips**. Navigate to the Movies folder on the CD-ROM that came with this book.

6. Select "**Butterfly Movie**," then click **Import**.

7. Give the movie the name "**Butterfly**." Click **Play** to see it. Click **OK**.

8. Choose **Insert Clip**, then close the window.

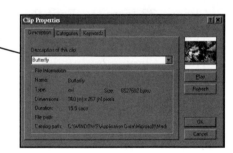

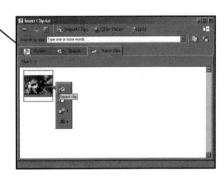

9. Go to **Playing the Movie** section on the next page.

Inserting a Movie into a File   98 & 97 only

3. Choose **Movie** from the **Insert** menu.

4. Navigate to the **Movies** folder on the CD-ROM that came with this book.

5. Double-click the **Movies** folder.

6. Double-click the **"Butterfly Movie"** file.

7. Place the movie so it is **centered on the page**.

Playing the Movie

1. Windows users **click the movie** to play.

2. Macintosh users **click the "filmstrip"** icon on the movie, then click the **Play** button on the strip.

Saving the File

The movie file must be loaded on the computer or the movie won't play. It's a good idea to place the file and the movie in the same folder.

1. **Create a folder** named "**Butterfly files**" on your hard drive.

2. **Copy** the "**Butterfly**" movie **into** the **folder**.

3. Go back to the "**Butterfly**" file you have open in *Word*.

4. Choose **Save As** from the **File** menu and save the file in the newly created folder.

Windows

Butterflies play an important part in pollination of plants. Butterflies, like other insects are attracted to flowers by color and scent. The butterfly gets food from nectar or nutrient-rich pollen, or both. The most common insect pollinators are beetles, flies, butterflies, moths, and bees.

There are more than 170,000 kinds of butterflies and moths. They are known as Lepidoptera, which means "scale wing." Their wings are covered with thousands of tiny scales that give the wings their beautiful colors. Most butterflies fly all day and have brightly colored wings that close together over their backs when they are resting. They have a slim body and thin antennae with clubbed ends which are used for smelling.

Most moths are dull in color. They fly at night, have feathery or hairy antennae, and a stout and hairy body. A moth holds its wings open when it is resting. A moth's front wing is often linked to its back wing on each side by tiny hairs that act like hooks.

Macintosh

Butterflies play an important part in pollination of plants. Butterflies, like other insects are attracted to flowers by color and scent. The butterfly gets food from nectar or nutrient-rich pollen, or both. The most common insect pollinators are beetles, flies, butterflies, moths, and bees.

There are more than 170,000 kinds of butterflies and moths. They are known as Lepidoptera, which means "scale wing." Their wings are covered with thousands of tiny scales that give the wings their beautiful colors. Most butterflies fly all day and have brightly colored wings that close together over their backs when they are resting. They have a slim body and thin antennae with clubbed ends which are used for smelling.

Most moths are dull in color. They fly at night, have feathery or hairy antennae, and a stout and hairy body. A moth holds its wings open when it is resting. A moth's front wing is often linked to its back wing on each side by tiny hairs that act like hooks.

Internet Pictures in a Report

Create a Worksheet with Internet Pictures

It is easy to include graphics from the Internet in *Word* documents. All you do is copy the picture from the Internet and paste it into the *Word* file. Not all browsers allow you to copy and paste a picture, but you can save the pictures and insert them later. Both methods are shown below.

> ### This Activity Covers the Following Topics
> * Copying an Image
> * Pasting an Image
> * Downloading the Image

Copying an Image

1. Open "Polar Bear Report" from the CD-ROM that came with this book. You're going to put an Internet picture of a polar bear under the paragraph.

2. **Open Internet Explorer** or **other browser**. If you don't have enough memory to have both *Word* and the browser open, quit *Word* and open your browser. You can open *Word* after you copy the picture.

3. **Type the address of a Web site** and press ⏎ (Windows) ⏎ (Macintosh). (http://www.omahazoo.com has a great picture.)

4. Scroll through the site until you **find a picture** that will work with the report.

5. **Right-click** (Macintosh users click and hold) **the picture**. A box of choices will appear. **Note:** If your browser won't do this, skip to the Downloading the Image section below.

6. **Drag** to **Copy Image**. You won't see anything happen, but the picture will be copied into the clipboard of the computer.

7. Click in the **Taskbar** at the bottom of the screen to choose *Word* (Macintosh users choose *Word* from the application icon in the upper right corner of your screen), or launch it again.

Pasting an Image

1. Press ⌃Ⓥ (Windows) ⌘Ⓥ (Macintosh) or choose **Paste** from the **Edit** menu.

2. **Move the picture** to the **center of the page**.

Downloading the Image

You may need to save the image to a disk instead of copying it into the clipboard.

1. Choose **Download Image to Disk** instead of **Copy Image**.

2. With the "Polar Bear Report" open, choose **Picture**, then **From File** from the **Insert** menu.

Be sure to cite the source of your picture. You can type the Web address in a text box. If you need help, turn to page 81.

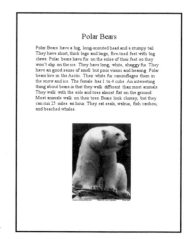

AutoShapes

Use AutoShapes in Your Documents

Word has all kinds of geometric shapes built into the program for your use. It also has arrows, banners, conversation balloons, flowchart symbols, and basic drawing tools. Once you've drawn the shapes, you can add shadows, 3-D effects, and color. The flexibility of these tools is amazing!

This Activity Covers the Following Topics

- Creating an Arrow
- Rotating the Arrow
- Creating a Banner
- Drawing a Basic Shape
- Changing the Color of an AutoShape
- Creating a Shadowed Shape
- Creating a 3-D Shape
- Formatting a 3-D Shape
- Adding Multiple AutoShapes

Creating an Arrow

1. Create a new *Word* document.

2. Choose **AutoShapes** from the **Drawing** toolbar, or choose **Picture**, then **AutoShapes** from the **Insert** menu.

3. Choose **Block Arrows** and **drag to the right** until the palette tears off and stays on the screen.

4. Click the **Curved Down Arrow** shape.

5. Place the + shaped cursor on the upper left corner of the page. **Click and drag** to draw the arrow.

Rotating the Arrow

1. Click the **Free Rotate** icon on the **Drawing** toolbar .

2. Place the cursor on the **upper right handle**. **Drag the handle down** to change the direction of the arrow.

3. **Click in the white area** around the arrow to deselect the rotate cursor function. **Click the arrow** to select it, then **click the first yellow diamond** and **drag right** to make the arrow thinner.

Creating a Banner

1. Choose **Stars and Banners** from **AutoShapes** and drag the palette onto the page.

2. Click the **Up Ribbon** shape.

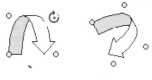

3. Place the + shaped cursor on the upper left corner of the page. **Click and drag** to draw the banner across the page.

4. Click the **Text Box** icon 📧 and draw a text box across the center of the banner.

5. Type "**Congratulations.**" Adjust the font size, text alignment, and font color to make it look great.

Drawing a Basic Shape

1. Choose **Basic Shapes** from **AutoShapes** and drag the palette onto the page.

2. Click the **Moon** shape.

3. Place the **+** shaped cursor on the upper left corner of the page. **Click and drag** to draw a moon on the page.

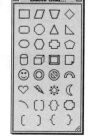

Changing the Color of an AutoShape

1. Click the **Moon** shape.

2. Click the **Fill Color** arrow on the **Drawing** toolbar.

3. Click **More Fill Colors.**

4. Choose a **Yellow** color. Click **OK**.

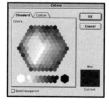

Creating a Shadowed Shape

1. Click the **Shadow** icon.

2. **Click a shadow.**

Creating a 3-D Shape

1. Draw another **Basic Shape** (a flat one, not a 3-D one).

2. **Fill the shape** with a **color.**

3. Click the **3-D** icon.

4. Click a **3-D shape.**

Formatting a 3-D Shape

1. Click the **3-D icon**, then choose **3-D Settings**.

2. Click the arrow next to the **3-D Color** icon.

3. **Click a color** or click More 3-D Colors for more choices.

Sometimes it's hard to see the 3-D effect because of the color. Experiment with colors and other 3-D settings to get just the effect you want.

Adding Multiple AutoShapes

1. **Double-click** the **Triangle. Draw a small triangle.**

2. Notice that the cursor is still a **+**. This means you can keep drawing triangles until you click another shape. **Draw two more triangles.**

3. **Click elsewhere on the page.** A triangle is drawn every time you click. **Draw a few more triangles on the page by clicking.** Click the **Arrow** on the **Drawing** toolbar, then drag to move the triangles.

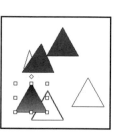

Insert a Table

Create a Rubric and an Assignment Sheet

In every class there are a few kids who need a little help getting organized. Creating a table is an easy way to make a rubric and an assignment sheet for them.

> ### This Activity Covers the Following Topics
> - Setting Up the Page
> - Creating a Table
> - Setting Row Height
> - Adding Text
> - Drawing a Row
> - Inserting Symbols
> - Saving the File
> - Setting Up the WordArt Heading
> - Formatting the WordArt
> - Drawing the Name Line
> - Drawing the Table
> - Distributing the Columns & Rows
> - Entering Text in the Table
> - Adding Clip Art

Setting Up the Page

Rubrics are frequently laid out on a horizontal page.

1. Create a new *Word* **document.**

Windows

2. Choose **Page Setup** from the **File** menu.

3. Type ".5" for each margin.

4. Click the **Paper Size** tab.

5. Click the **Landscape** radio button. Click **OK**.

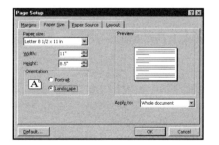

Macintosh

2. Choose **Document** from the **Format** menu.

3. Type ".5" for each margin.

4. Click the **Page Setup** button.

5. Click the **Landscape** icon next to **Orientation**.

6. Click **OK**, then **OK** again.

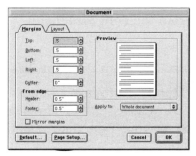
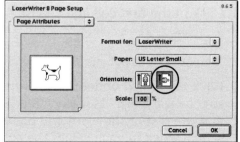

Creating a Table

1. Choose **75%** from the **Zoom Control box** so you can see the entire page.

2. Click the **Insert Table** icon 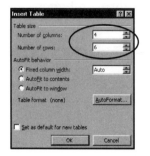 and drag to choose **4 Columns** and **6 Rows**. **Hint:** If it stops at 4 x 5, hold the mouse button down for a moment and then drag again to increase the number of columns and rows.

    or

    Choose **Insert Table** from the **Table** menu.

    Type "**4**" in **Number of Columns** and "**6**" in **Number of Rows**. Click **OK**.

Setting Row Height

2000 only

1. Click in the first cell and drag to **Select** the entire table.

2. Choose **Table Properties** from the **Table** menu.

3. Click the **Row** tab.

4. Click the box next to **Specify Height**, then type "**1**" in the larger box.

5. Click to **remove the check mark** from **Allow row to break across pages**.

6. Click **OK**. (Continue at number 7 below.)

98 & 97 only

1. Press [CTRL][A] (Windows) [⌘][A] (Macintosh) or choose **Select All** from the **Edit** menu to select the entire table.

2. Choose **Cell Height and Width** from the **Table** menu.

3. Click the **Row** tab.

4. Type "**70**" in the **At** box.

5. Click to **remove the check mark** from **Allow row to break across pages**.

6. Click **OK**.

7. Move the cursor to the **line between rows one and two**. The cursor changes to a crosshair ⚊ .

8. **Drag to move the line down** until the row is **almost twice as tall**.

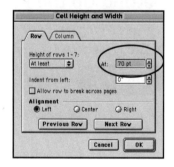

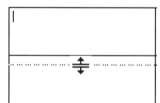

Adding Text

1. Click in the **first cell** and choose **48** from the **Font Size** menu.

2. Type "**Day**."

3. Select the rest of the rows and choose "**24**" from the **Font Size** menu.

4. Click in the **cell under** "**Day**." Type "**Mond**." **AutoText** assumes that you're going to type the word "Monday." Since you are, press [ENTER] (Windows) [RETURN] (Macintosh) and the rest of the word will be typed for you. Type the remaining days of the school week in each cell of the column.

Drawing a Row

1. Click the **Tables and Borders icon** and draw a line to divide the last three columns of the top row. Click the **Pencil** tool on the Tables and Borders toolbar to deselect it.

2. Select the bottom row that you just created. Choose "**24**" from the **Font Size** menu and center the text.

3. Type "**On task 80% of the time**" in the first box. Type "**On task 50-80% of the time**" in the middle box, and "**On task less than 50% of the time**" in the last box.

Day			

Day			
	On task 80% of the time	On task 50-80% of the time	On task less than 50% of the time

Inserting Symbols

1. Select the top three rows you just created. **Center** the text and make it **48** pt.

2. Click in the first new cell (above On task 80% of the time). Choose **Symbol** from the **Insert** menu.

3. Choose **Wingdings** from the **Font** menu in that window.

4. Find the **Happy Face** symbol and click **Insert.**

5. Insert the other face symbols in the columns to the right.

Day	☺	☺	☹
	On Task 80% of the time	On task 50-80% of the time	On task less than 50% of the time
Monday			
Tuesday			
Wednesday			
Thursday			
Friday			

Saving the File

All right! **Save** the file on your hard drive or floppy disk and **Print** it.

Tables can also be drawn. The steps below will help you create an assignment sheet.

Setting Up the WordArt Heading

1. Create a new *Word* document.

2. Press ⏎ (Windows) ⏎ (Macintosh) seven times.

3. Click the **Insert WordArt icon** or choose **Picture**, then **WorkArt** from the **Insert** menu. Double-click a style.

4. Type "**Assignments**" and click **OK**. Drag it to the top.

5. Use the same WordArt style and type the word "**for.**"

Formatting the WordArt

1. Click the **WordArt** shape icon in the WordArt toolbar.

2. Click the **straight line** shape.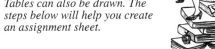

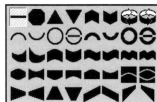

Drawing the Name Line

1. From the Drawing toolbar, click the **Straight Line** icon and **draw a line** under the word **for.**

2. Choose a **wider line** from the **Line Style** icon.

Drawing the Table

1. Click the **Draw Table** icon or choose **Draw Table** from the **Table** menu.

2. Using the pencil tool, **draw a box under the heading**.

3. **Draw horizontal lines** to create **7 rows**. Make the first row much smaller than the rest.

4. Draw **vertical lines** to create **6 columns**.

The rows and columns aren't even. We'll fix that next.

Distributing the Columns & Rows

1. Move the cursor to the **second row outside of the table on the left side**. It changes to an arrow. Click and **drag down to select all the rows**.

2. Click the **Distribute Rows Evenly** icon from the **Tables and Borders** palette.

3. Click the **Distribute Columns Evenly** icon.

Entering Text in the Table

1. Click in the **top left cell**. Type "**Assignment.**"

2. Press [TAB] to move to the cell on the right. Type the **days of the week** in the first row.

3. **Select** the entire row. **Boldface** the text. Click the **Center** button.

4. Choose **Borders and Shading** from the **Format** menu.

5. Click the **Shading** tab and select a **light** color. Click **OK**.

6. **Select all the rows**. Click the **Center** button. This centers the text in the middle of the cells.

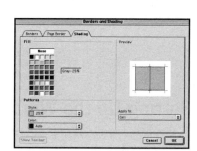

Assignment	Monday	Tuesday	Wednesday	Thursday	Friday

Adding Clip Art

Adding pictures to the assignment sheet can make it more appealing to kids.

1. In version 2000, draw a **Text Box** in a cell where you'd like to insert clip art (this lets you predetermine placement and allows you to move it as a graphic). Earlier versions skip to the next step.

2. Click the **Clip Art** icon or choose **Picture**, then **Clip Art** from the **Insert** menu.

3. Insert clip art **for each Assignment**.

Reading

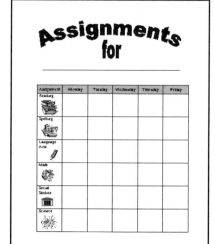

Footnotes

Use Footnotes in a Letter

We struggled to make footnotes with typewriters but it's so easy to make them with *Word.*
Footnotes aren't just used in term papers, they can also be used in letters to insert information.

This Activity Covers the Following Topics
- Inserting a Footnote
- Removing a Footnote

Inserting a Footnote

1. Open the file "Field Trip Letter" from the CD-ROM that came with this book. The activity on page 25 uses this file to teach users to edit a *Word* file. You may complete that activity first, or use this file as it is.

2. Click at the **end** of the word **Zoo** because that's where you want the first footnote number to appear. You're going to write the address for the zoo as a footnote.

3. Choose **Footnote** from the **Insert** menu. The Footnote section gives you choices about the location and numbering of footnotes. Click **OK**.

   The number "1" appears in superscript above the second "o" in Zoo. Subsequent notes are numbered in sequence.

> We're going on a field trip May 20! The kids have been working very hard learning about the animal kingdom. They have researched where animal live, about their family, and their hunting and feeding habits. Now it's time to see some of these animals up close. We will visit the Lied Jungle at Henry Doorly Zoo[1] and Educational Service Unit #3's Gifford Farm.[2] Would you like to go with us?

At the same time, *Word* drops the text cursor into the footnote panel, inserts the note number, and leaves the cursor blinking.

4. In the footnote panel, **type the text of the first footnote in the screen shot to the right**. All the edit, revise, copy, and paste techniques you use in ordinary text apply in the footnote panel.

5. When you have finished the note, **click anywhere in the letter** to resume work on the main document.

6. Click after the period following the words "**Gifford Farm.**" Choose **Footnote** from the **Insert** menu. **Type** the **second footnote** shown in the **screen shot above**.

Removing a Footnote

1. In the text, select the **reference number** of the **first footnote**.

2. Press **Delete**. *Word* removes the note, rearranges the pages, and renumbers remaining notes in the text and in the footnote panel.

Leading in a Document

Tighten Up the Text

The leading (pronounced like lead in a pencil) is the white space between lines of text. This can be changed to make a document more compact or to expand it on a page. If you have a document that won't quite fit on one page, and it has to be a single-page document, tightening up the leading can make it fit on one page.

> ### This Activity Covers the Following Topic
> • Changing the Leading

Changing the Leading

1. Open the file "Field Trip Letter" from the CD-ROM that came with this book.

2. Highlight the **first paragraph**.

3. Choose **Paragraph** from the **Format** menu.

4. Click the **Indents and Spacing** tab.

5. The paragraph dialog box appears. The default of line spacing is **Single**. Click the arrow under **Line spacing:** and choose **Exactly**.

6. Click the **Down Arrow** under **At:** to choose **11 pt**.

7. Click **OK**.

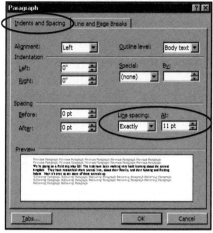

The first paragraph in the screen shot below is still in 12 pt. Times, but the leading has been changed to 11 pt. The second paragraph still has **Single** line spacing. Notice how much closer the lines are in the first paragraph compared to the second paragraph.

> Dear Parents:
>
> We're going on a field trip May 20! The kids have been working very hard learning about the animal kingdom. They have researched where animals live, about their family, and their hunting and feeding habits. Now it's time to see some of these animals up close. We will visit the Lied Jungle at Henry Doorly Zoo and Educational Service Unit #3's Gifford Farm. Would you like to go with us?
>
> Both Mrs. Fischer's and Mr. Harper's classes will be going on this day-long field trip. We would like to have one sponsor for every five students, so we need ten parent volunteers. Students have a great time learning about animals on this field trip so you'll have a great time, too.

When you are changing leading, you would be wise to vary the leading only one or two points at a time. Check to make sure the tops (ascenders) and bottoms (descenders) of each letter are showing, especially capital letters and the lower part of letters, e.g., "g."

Envelopes & Labels

Create Envelopes the Easy Way

Why should you use *Word* to create a great-looking letter and then handwrite the envelope? You don't have to—just use the *Word's* Labels and Envelopes feature to print the envelopes!

This Activity Covers the Following Topics
- Creating the Delivery Address
- Creating the Return Address
- Creating an Envelope from a Letter
- Creating a Label

Creating the Delivery Address

1. Create a new *Word* document.

2. Choose **Envelopes and Labels** from the **Tools** menu.

3. Click the **Envelopes** tab.

4. **Type the name and address** of the person you're sending the letter to in the **Delivery Address** box.

Creating the Return Address

1. Type your name and address in the **Return Address** box.

2. Click **Print**.

3. Click **Yes** if you want the return address to appear each time you create an envelope. Click **No** if you want to create the address each time.

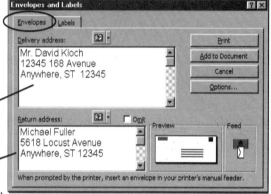

Creating an Envelope from a Letter

1. Create a new *Word* document.

2. Type a letter including the **inside address**.

3. Choose **Envelopes and Labels** from the **Tools** menu. The inside address from the letter will be visible in the **Delivery Address** box.

4. Click **Cancel** to close the window.

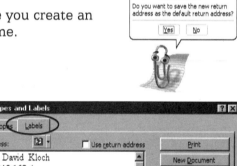

Creating a Label

1. Choose **Envelopes and Labels** from the **Tools** menu.

2. Click the **Labels** tab.

3. Click **Print**. A sheet of labels will be printed. To print one, click **Single label**.

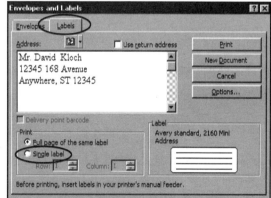

Merged Letter

Merge Names & Addresses in a Letter

You can create a personalized letter for every student by using the merge element of *Word*. Here's how to create a data source and merge it into a letter to parents.

> ### This Activity Covers the Following Topics
> * Inserting AutoText
> * Creating a Mail Merge Document
> * Creating the Main Document (Step 1)
> * Creating the Data Source (Step 2)
> * Editing the Data Source
> * Completing the Main Document (Step 3)
> * Previewing the Merged Document
> * Merging to an Envelope

Inserting AutoText

1. Open the file "Science Fair Letter" from the CD-ROM that came with this book. It reads strangely because there are blanks where words from the data source will be merged.

2. Click the cursor two spaces below the words "I am so proud of !"

3. Choose **AutoText**, then **Closing**, then **Sincerely** from the **Insert** menu.

4. Type **your name** where it reads **Teacher Name.**

Creating a Mail Merge Document

The "Science Fair Letter" needs to be sent to all students who were picked to go to the Regional Science Fair. You don't need to type the same information into all of them and address each letter. Mail merge will do this for you. Mail merge takes four steps.

Creating the Main Document (Step 1)

1. Choose **Mail Merge** from the **Tools** menu.

2. Choose **Form Letters** from the **Main Document** menu.

3. Choose **Active Window** to indicate you want the current file **"Science Fair Letter"** to be the document you use as a merge document.

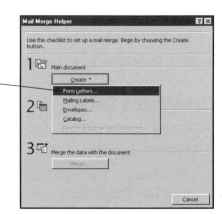

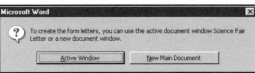

Creating the Data Source (Step 2)

You're going to create a list (Data Source) of names, addresses, and phone numbers for your students. This information will be merged with the Science Fair letter.

A data source contains fields and records. A **field** is a category name, e.g., First Name. There can be several different fields in a data source. A **record** is all of the information about one person. This information will be merged into the main document (in this case, Science Fair Letter) modified in Step 1. A data source can be used in any document once you have created it.

1. Choose **Create Data Source** from the **Data Source** menu.

   Word provides a list of commonly used fields. Scroll down to familiarize yourself with the field names. Five of the names are not needed for this activity so you'll remove them.

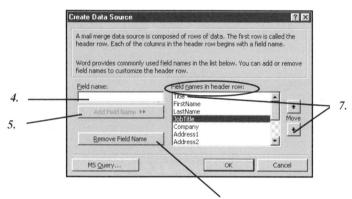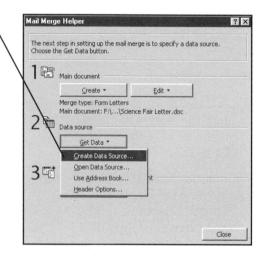

2. Click the field name **JobTitle.** Click **Remove Field Name** because it won't be needed in this data source.

3. Remove the field names **Company**, **WorkNumber**, **Address2**, and **Country.**

4. Type "**StudentFirst**" in the **Field Name** box. **Note:** No spaces are allowed in field names.

5. Click **Add Field Name.**

6. Add the field name **StudentLast.**

7. Click the field name **Title.** Click the **down arrow** on the right side of the box. This will move it to the bottom of the **Field names in header row** box.

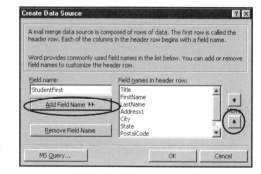

8. Using the up and down arrows, put the field names in this order: **StudentFirst, StudentLast, Address1, City, State, PostalCode, HomePhone, Title, FirstName, LastName.** Click **OK.**

9. Name the file "**Student Data**" and save it on your hard drive or floppy disk.

Editing the Data Source

1. A message telling you there are no data records appears. Click **Edit Data Source** to add student records.

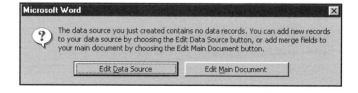

2. Enter data for **5 students** including the names **Michelle Chan**, **Deon Peterson**, and **Juan Martinez**. Press [TAB] to move from field to field. Click **Add New** to add a new name.

3. Click **View Source** when you have added 5 names.

4. **Check your data**. You can make changes in this view.

5. Click the **Move Table Column** icon to widen the **Address1** column.

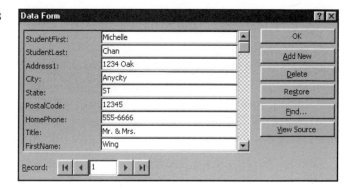

6. Click in the **StudentLast** column. Click the **Sort Ascending** button to sort the records by last name.

7. Click the **Save** icon to save the data source. Name the file **"Student Records"** and save it on your hard drive or floppy disk.

8. Click the **Mail Merge Main Document** icon to return to the "Science Fair Letter" file. Now you're ready for Step 3, entering the merge fields into the letter.

Completing the Main Document (Step 3)

1. **Place the cursor to the left of the colon** in the greeting.

2. Choose **Title** from the **Insert Merge Field** menu. The field data indicator shows a merge has been done.

> Dear «Title» «FirstName» «LastName»:
>
> Your child , has been chosen to represent Lincoln

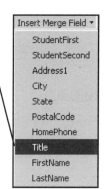

3. Press the **Spacebar** and **merge** the field **FirstName**.

4. Press the **Spacebar** and **merge** the field **LastName**.

5. Click to place the cursor to the left of the comma after "**Your child,**" in the first line.

6. Merge **StudentFirst** in this space.

7. Merge **StudentFirst** in the last sentence of the first paragraph (see the screen shot).

8. Merge **StudentFirst** in the last line before the closing, "**I am so proud of !**" (see the screen shot).

Dear «Title» «FirstName» «LastName»:

Your child, «StudentFirst», has been chosen to represent Lincoln Middle School in the Midwest Regional Science Fair to be held in Chicago on April 23-24, 2000. This is a great honor and «StudentFirst» is to be congratulated.

Students will be driven in a school van at 8:00 every morning and will return at 3:00. Please send a sack lunch or provide lunch money every day. Return the signed permission form by Friday and call if you have any questions.

I am so proud of «StudentFirst»!

Sincerely,

9. Scroll down to the permission form and merge **StudentFirst** at the beginning of the first sentence. Press the **Spacebar**.

«StudentFirst» has my permission to attend the the Midwest Regional Science Fair to be held in Chicago on April 23-24, 2000.

Daytime phone _____

Signature _____

Previewing the Merged Document

1. Click the **View Merged Document** icon.

2. The letter with the names for the first record instead of field data indicators appears. **Scroll down** to look at the **permission form.**

3. Click the **Next Record** button to see the data for the next record inserted into the letter.

4. Click the **Last Record** button to see the data for the last record inserted into the letter.

5. Click the **Find Record** button.

6. Type "**Deon**" and click **Find First**. The data in Deon's record appears in the letter. Click **Close.**

7. Click the **Merge to Printer** button. Deon's data will be merged and a letter will be printed. This method of merging data keeps the original letter separate from the data.

Dear Mr. & Mrs. Wing Chan:

Your child, Michelle, has been chosen to represent Lincoln Middle School in the Midwest Regional Science Fair to be held in Chicago on April 23-24, 2000. This is a great honor and Michelle is to be congratulated.

Students will be driven in a school van at 8:00 every morning and will return at 3:00. Please send a sack lunch or provide lunch money every day. Return the signed permission form by Friday and call if you have any questions.

I am so proud of Michelle!

Sincerely,

Be sure your Field Name matches the data you are typing in "Find what." If you type a student's last name in the "Find what" box and the In Field reads StudentFirst, Word won't be able to find the record!

Merging to an Envelope

1. Choose **Mail Merge** from the **Tools** menu.

2. Choose **Envelope** from the **Merge Document** menu.

3. Choose **New Main Document.**

4. Choose **Open Data Source** from the **Get Data** menu.

5. Navigate to the Student Records file.

6. Click **Set Up Main Document**.

7. Click **OK** in the **Envelope Options** window.

8. Choose the fields for the delivery address from the **Insert Merge Field** menu.

9. Click **OK**, then **Close.**

The envelope appears. Your return address appears if you have set it up in the Envelopes and Labels option. Click the **View Merged Document** icon to see the merged data.

Outline View

Create an Outline

Outlines allow information to be organized in a logical, easy-to-grasp manner. *Word* not only makes outlining a simple process, it offers a variety of styles to choose from.

This Activity Covers the Following Topics
- Using the Outline View
- Viewing in the Print Layout View
- Adding the Outline Numbers

Using the Outline View

1. Create a new *Word* document.

2. Click the **Outline icon** or choose **Outline** from the **View** menu.

3. **Type the text in the screen shot. Press** the [ENTER] (Windows) [RETURN] (Macintosh) key or buttons as **directed on the screen shot.**

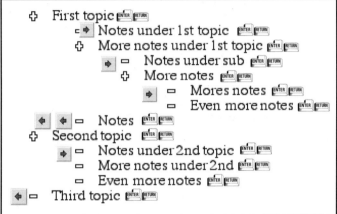

Viewing in the Print Layout View

Click the **Print Layout icon** or choose **Print Layout** (Page Layout in *Word* 98 & *Word* 97) from the **View** menu. The text is no longer in Outline view. You'll fix this next.

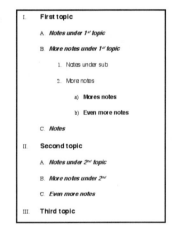

Adding the Outline Numbers

1. Choose **Bullets and Numbering** from the **Format** menu.

2. Click the **Outline Numbered** tab, then the format that looks like a typical outline. Click **OK**.

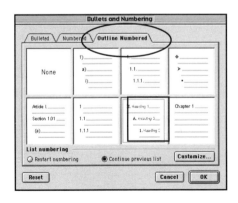

Outlines can be converted directly into PowerPoint slides. Choose Send To, then Microsoft PowerPoint from the File menu.

Create a Custom Outline

Create an Outline That Exactly Meets Your Needs

The default outline style in *Word* may not exactly meet your needs. You can create an outline style that looks exactly the way you want it to. You can also create key commands to indent text. It takes several steps to create, but it will look just like you want and be easy to use. Try it and see what you think!

> ### This Activity Covers the Following Topics
> - Creating the Outline
> - Editing the Style
> - Creating a Shortcut
> - Creating the Second Line of the Outline
> - Testing the New Styles
> - Finishing the Editing of Styles

Creating the Outline

1. Create a new *Word* document.

2. Choose **Bullets and Numbering** from the **Format** menu.

3. Click the **Outline Numbered** tab, then the format that looks like a typical outline. Click **OK**. The style box reads **Heading 1** and "**I.**" appears in the document.

4. Type "**First topic**."

Editing the Style

When you edit a style, you have the option of assigning a key command to that style. Key commands are generally considered to be faster than mousing because you don't have to move your hands from the keyboard to the mouse and then back to the keyboard again. Traditional outlines don't use bold and italics as the built-in outlines do in *Word*. You'll change that.

1. Because **Heading 1** is the style you are using, this is the style you will edit. Choose **Style** from the **Format** menu.

2. Click **New**.

3. Give the style the name "**Outline 1,**" then click **Format** and choose **Font**.

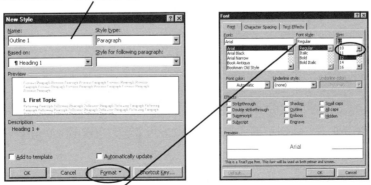

4. Choose **Regular** from **Font styles**, then choose **12** from the **Size** menu. Click **OK**.

5. Click **Format**, then **Paragraph**.

6. Click the **Up Arrow** on the **Before** box to choose **6 pt.**

7. Click the **Up Arrow** on the **After** box to choose **0 pt.** Click **OK.**

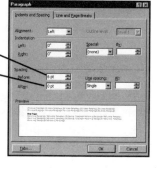

Creating a Shortcut

It will be much easier to use this style if you can use a shortcut instead of clicking in the Heading menu. You're going to set your own shortcut keys.

1. Click **Shortcut Key**.

2. Press 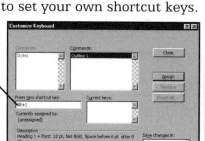 (Windows) (Macintosh). Click **Assign**, then **Close**.

3. Click **Add to template,** then **OK**.

4. Click **Apply**.

Creating the Second Line of the Outline

1. Choose **Heading 2** from the **Style box**.

2. Type "**Notes under 1st topic.**"

3. **Edit** the style following the steps above. Name the style **Outline 2**. Make the shortcut keys [ALT]2 (Windows) [CTRL]2 (Macintosh).

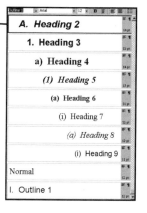

Testing the New Styles

1. Click in the **first line of your outline**.

2. **Press** [ALT][2] (Windows) [CTRL][2] (Macintosh). The text will move to the second indent position.

3. **Press** [ALT][1] (Windows) [CTRL][1] (Macintosh). The cursor will move to the first position.

4. Create a **new** *Word* document.

5. **Press** [ALT][1] (Windows) [CTRL][1] (Macintosh). The format for your first line of the outline appears. Type "**First topic**" and press [ENTER] (Windows) [RETURN] (Macintosh).

6. **Press** [ALT][2] (Windows) [CTRL][2] (Macintosh). The format for the second line appears.

Finishing the Editing of Styles

1. **Press** [ENTER] (Windows) [RETURN] (Macintosh).

2. Choose **Heading 3** from the **Style box** and type "**Notes under sub.**"

3. **Edit the style.** Name it **Outline 3**. Assign the shortcut keys [ALT][3] (Windows) [CTRL][3] (Macintosh).

4. **Press** [ENTER] (Windows) [RETURN] (Macintosh).

5. Choose **Heading 4** from the **Style box** and type "**More notes.**"

6. **Edit the style.** Name it **Outline 4**. Assign the shortcut keys [ALT][4] (Windows) [CTRL][4] (Macintosh).

Letterheads

Create Your Own Stationery

It's easy to make attractive and professional-looking letterhead stationery using *Word*. Follow these directions to make your own!

> ### This Activity Covers the Following Topics
> - Changing the Margins
> - Inserting a Text Box
> - Inserting WordArt
> - Inserting Clip Art
> - Saving as a Template
> - Using a Template

Changing the Margins

Letterhead text and graphics do not start 1" from the top of the page in stationery you buy. Instead, they usually start closer to the top. The default *Word* document has 1" top and bottom margins and 1.5" side margins. The first thing to do when creating letterhead is to change the margins.

1. Create a new *Word* document.

2. Choose **Page Setup** from the **File** menu (Macintosh users choose **Document** from the **Format** menu).

3. Give the document a **Top** margin of **.5"** and side margins of **1"**. Click **OK**.

   Note: You can also drag the left margin markers to the left to change margins.

4. Press ⌨ENTER (Windows) ⌨RETURN (Macintosh) **10** times to move the cursor down. The space above the carriage returns will contain the letterhead text and graphics. You'll begin typing at the cursor location. This can be modified later if needed.

Inserting a Text Box

1. Click the **Text Box** icon 🔲 or choose **Text Box** from the **Insert** menu.

2. Hold the mouse button down and drag to **draw a text box** in the upper left corner of the page.

3. Type "**Notes from**" in the text box.

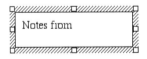

4. Triple-click or drag to **select the text**. Choose **18** from the **Font Size** box 🔲.

5. The text box is outlined with a thin line. You're going to remove it. Click the arrow next to the **Line Color icon** 🖊 and choose **No Line**.

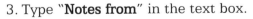

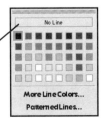

Special letterheads for students to use can be created to motivate them, e.g., spelling lists, math worksheets, etc.

Inserting WordArt

1. Click the **WordArt icon** 4 or choose **Picture**, then **WordArt** from the **Insert** menu.

2. Double-click a **WordArt style** you like.

3. Type **your name** in the highlighted text box. Click **OK**.

4. Click the **Arrow** tool. Drag the two elements to an attractive arrangement.

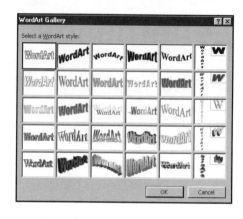

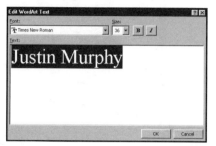

Notes from

Justin Murphy

Inserting Clip Art

1. Click outside of the text box, then click the **Clip Art icon** or choose **Picture**, then **Clip Art** from the **Insert** menu. The clip art palette appears. When Microsoft *Office* or *Word* is installed, a small number of clip art images are loaded. There are tons of good clip art images on the *Office* CD-ROM that is not loaded. You must have the *Office* CD-ROM in the drive to access these images.

Most schools purchase Office without buying a CD-ROM for each computer. In order to use all the images, you need to borrow the CD-ROM from the computer administrator or ask to have the clip art images loaded on your computer or on a server.

2000 only

2. Click a **folder** image, e.g., **Academic**. Clip art with a matching theme will appear providing a palette of choices. Click the **image you wish to use**.

3. A graphic menu appears. Click the **top choice** to insert the clip art, then close the window (click the X) in the title bar. You may click ← to go back to the previous screen.

Word 2000

Word 97 & 98

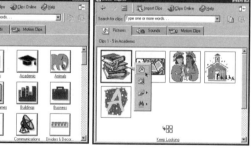
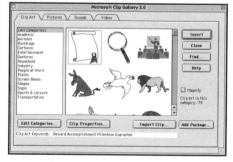

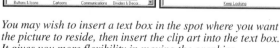

You may wish to insert a text box in the spot where you want the picture to reside, then insert the clip art into the text box. It gives you more flexibility in moving the graphics.

Notes from

Justin Murphy

98 & 97 only

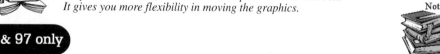

2. **Double-click an image** to insert it onto the page.

Saving As a Template

Word gives you the option of saving a file as a template. When you open a template, a copy of the original file is opened, preventing the original document from being altered.

1. Choose **Save As** from the **File** menu.

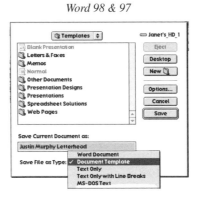

Word 2000   *Word 98 & 97*

2. Choose **Document Template** from the **Save File as Type** menu at the bottom of the window.

2000 only

3. Name the file. Click **Save**.

98 & 97 only

3. Double-click **Letters & Faxes**.

4. Name the file. Click **Save**.

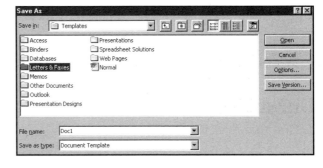

Note: Word 2000 users may navigate to the Templates folder if they want the template to be in the Office Templates folder.

Using a Template

1. Choose **New** from the **File** menu.

2. **Double-click the file** to open it. (Word 98 & 97 users click the Letters & Faxes tab first.)

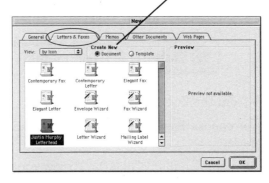

Screen Shots

Create a Computer Worksheet

Teachers make worksheets to help students through a computer process that requires many steps. They also make packets of self-paced learning exercises. Screen snapshots can make these worksheets easier to follow. This exercise will explain how to do it.

This Activity Covers the Following Topics

- Reading the Directions
- Drawing a Square
- Labeling the Screen Shot
- Creating Arrowhead Lines
- Printing the File

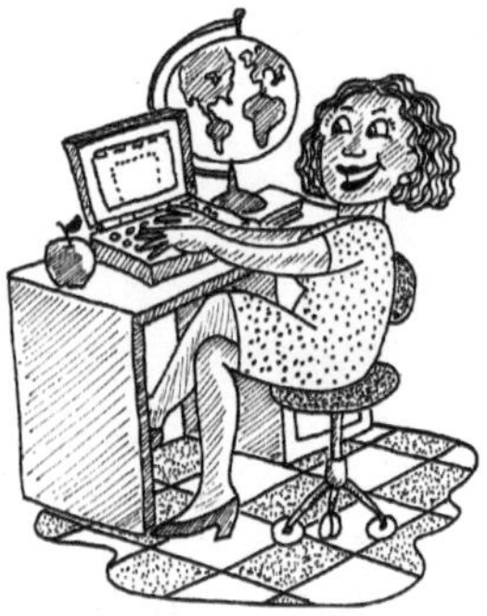

Reading the Directions

The "Square Worksheet" file is a worksheet that could be part of a self-paced packet to teach the drawing portion of *Word*. The worksheet is completed except for the snapshots to clarify the concepts. In this exercise you will add a screen snapshot in the middle of the document to finish the worksheet so it graphically shows students how to draw a perfect square.

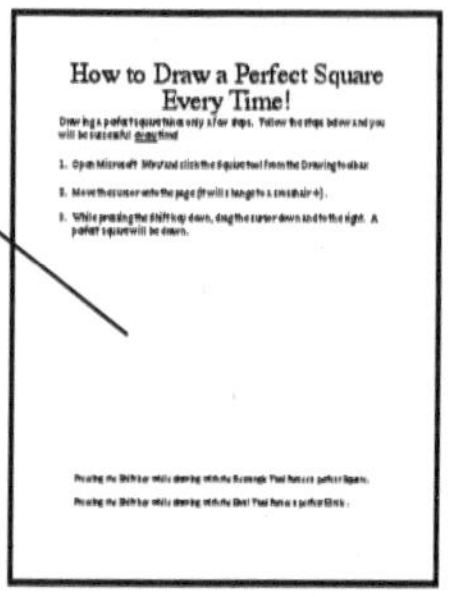

1. Open the file "Square Worksheet" from the CD-ROM that came with this book.
2. **Print** the worksheet and **read the directions**. *Don't close the file!*

Drawing a Square

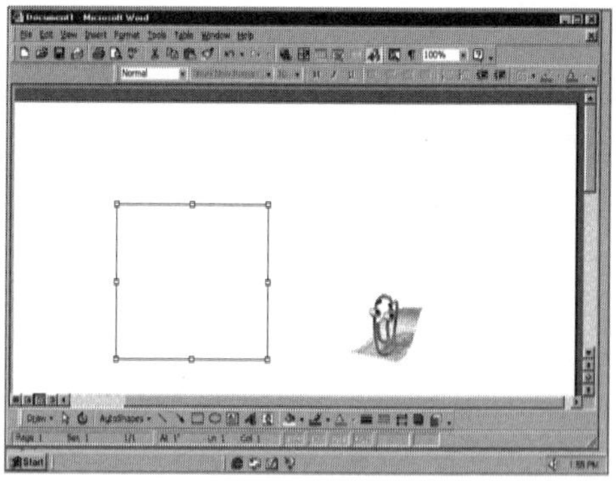

1. Create a new *Word* document.
2. **Read and follow the directions on the Square Worksheet page** you just printed. You'll create a perfect square on this document. You're going to make a screen shot of this screen after you draw the perfect square.

Windows

Now that you've drawn a square, you'll make a snapshot of this screen and insert it into the Square Worksheet file.

1. Press the **Print Screen** button on your keyboard. Nothing appears to happen, but the screen was copied into the clipboard of the computer.
2. Click "**Square Worksheet**" in the **Taskbar** at the bottom of the screen. The Square Worksheet file reappears.

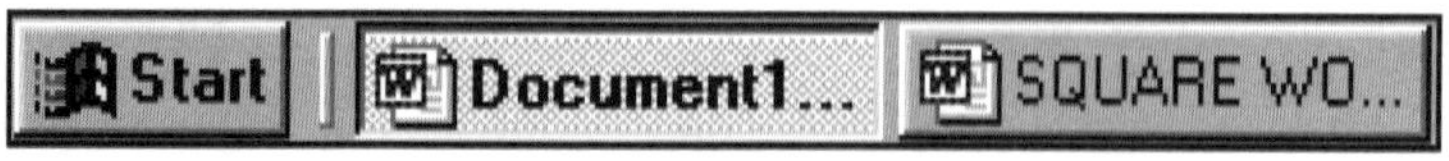

3. Choose **50%** from the **Zoom Box** 50%.
4. Press CTRL V or choose **Paste** from the **Edit** menu. The screen shot appears on the Square Worksheet page.
5. It needs to be made smaller. Click the **Arrow** tool and **drag a corner to shrink** it.

Macintosh

1. Macintosh users: Press 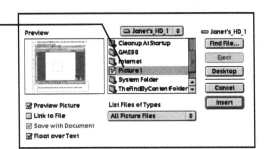. You'll hear a camera shutter sound to tell you that the screen was copied.

2. Choose "**Square Worksheet**" from the **Window** menu.

3. A file named "Picture 1" was created on the hard drive. Choose **Picture** then **From file** from the **Insert** menu.

4. Navigate to the hard drive and choose **Picture 1**.

5. The screen shot appears in the middle of the "Square Worksheet" page. It needs to be made smaller. Click the **Arrow** tool and drag to shrink the screen shot.

Macintosh users: If you press 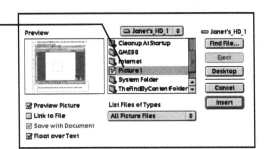, the cursor will change to a +. Then you can draw a box around the portion of the screen you want to snap. You don't have to snap the entire screen this way.

Labeling the Screen Shot

1. Click the **Text Box** icon 🔲 or choose **Text Box** from the **Insert** menu.

2. Hold the mouse button down and drag to **draw a text box to the left of the picture.**

3. Type "**Square Tool**" in the text box.

4. The text box is outlined with a thin line. Click the arrow next to the **Line Color icon** ✏️ and choose **No Line. Note:** If you need help, turn to the previous activity.

5. Using this method **create any other labels that would help users.**

Creating Arrowhead Lines

1. Click the **Arrow** tool 🖊️.

2. Draw a line from the label "**Square Tool**" to the tool.

3. Click the **Line Style** icon ▤ and choose **2 1/4 pt.**

4. **Draw arrows from the other labels** to their corresponding parts.

Printing the File

Print the file to see how cool it looks. Worksheets with screen shots and labels make teaching computer skills much easier.

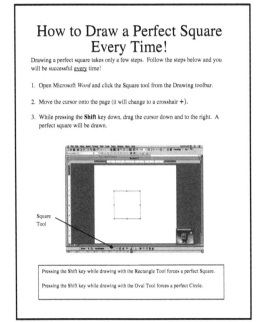

Create a Newsletter

Send a Newsletter Home Every Week

Newsletters are a terrific way to organize information in an attractive format. The *Word* Newsletter Assistant is a quick and easy way to make a newsletter template. It takes you step-by-step through the process of creating a standard newsletter. You can also create a newsletter on your own from scratch. You'll learn to create both in this activity.

> ### This Activity Covers the Following Topics
> - Changing the Margins
> - Setting the Columns
> - Viewing the Column Boundaries
> - Creating the Banner
> - Separating the Banner from the Text
> - Saving As a Template
> - Inserting the Stories
> - Formatting the Headings
> - Inserting Clip Art
> - Inserting a Watermark
> - Inserting a Border
> - Saving This Issue
> - Printing This Issue

Changing the Margins

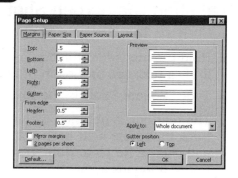

1. Create a new *Word* document.

   Newsletters never have large margins so the first thing you're going to do is to change the default margins.

2. Double-click in the left margin area.

   or

   Choose **Page Setup** from the **File** menu (Windows).

   Choose **Document** from the **Format** menu (Macintosh).

3. Click the **Margins** tab.

   or

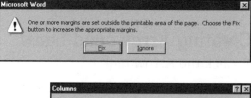

4. Choose .5" margins on all sides. If you see a warning that the margins are set outside the printable area, click **Ignore**.

Setting the Columns

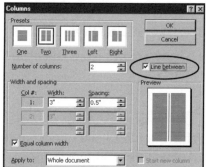

1. Click the **Columns** button ▦ and drag to choose **2 Columns**.

   or

   Choose **Columns** from the **Format** menu. Click **Two** and click **OK**. **Note:** You may click **Line Between** if you want a line separating the columns.

Viewing the Column Boundaries

1. Choose **Options** (Preferences in versions 98 & 97) from the **Tools** menu.

2. Click **Text Boundaries** and click **OK**.

The boundaries won't print; they're just to help you see where the columns are while you're writing.

Creating the Banner

1. Click the **Rectangle** tool ☐ on the **Draw** toolbar and draw a rectangle across the top of the page to mark the banner location.

2. Click the **WordArt** icon 📐 or choose **Picture,** then **WordArt** from the **Insert** menu. (Turn to page 82 for help on inserting WordArt.) Type the name of your newsletter, e.g., 5th Grade News.

3. Click the **Clip Art** icon 🖼 or choose **Picture,** then **Clip Art** from the **Insert** menu. (Turn to page 82 for help on inserting Clip Art.)

4. Click the **Text Box** icon 📧 or choose **Text Box** from the **Insert** menu. (Turn to page 81 for help on inserting a text box.) Draw a text box and type your professional name. Move it to the bottom of the banner.

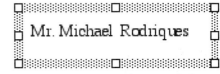

5. Click the **Line Color** icon 🖊 ▾ and choose **No Line.**

6. Create another text box. Choose **Date and Time** from the **Insert** menu. Choose a date style. **Note:** Be sure Update Automatically is not checked so the date won't change. You'll want to keep the date constant for this issue of the newsletter.

7. Insert or draw any other **graphics or text for the banner.**

8. Press |SHIFT| and click each element of the banner to select it.

9. Click the **Draw** menu Draw ▾ and choose **Group** 🗗 Group. The banner will show only 8 handles to indicate it is one object.

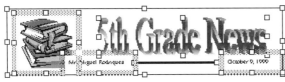 

If you start typing your newsletter stories now, they will move behind the banner. You need the banner to force the text to stay below it. You'll do that next.

Separating the Banner from the Text

2000 only

1. **Right-click** the banner (Macintosh users [CTRL] click) or choose **Format Object** from the **Format** menu.

2. Click the **Layout** tab and then **Square.**

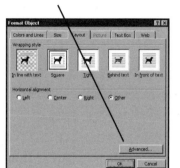 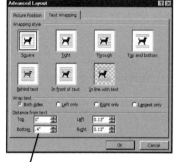 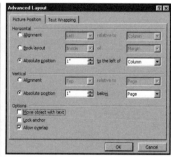

3. Click **Advanced.**

4. Click the **Text Wrapping** tab.

5. Type "**.4**" in the box next to **Bottom** to allow white space between the banner and the text.

6. Click the **Picture Position** tab.

7. Remove the check mark from **Move object with text.** Click **OK**, then **OK** again. (Move to number 6 below.)

98 & 97 only

1. **Right-click** the banner (Macintosh users [CTRL] click) or choose **Format Object** from the **Format** menu.

2. Click the **Wrapping** tab.

3. Choose **Square.**

4. Type "**.4**" in the box next to **Bottom.**

5. Click **OK.**

6. Click the insertion point so the cursor is below the banner.

7. Choose **Break** from the **Insert** menu.

8. Choose **Continuous** and click **OK.**

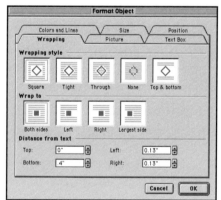

Saving As a Template

You are going to save this newsletter as a template document. Newsletters are ideal documents to save as templates so you can open up a blank document formatted as a newsletter. You'll be able to insert stories for this issue and save it without accidentally overwriting the previous issue.

1. Choose **Save As** from the **File** menu.

2. Give the file the name "**Newsletter.**"

Windows   *Macintosh*

3. Choose **Document Template** from the **Save as type** menu. The default place to save is in the *Word* Templates folder. You can save it in that folder, or choose a folder like Letters & Faxes.

Inserting the Stories

1. Open the file **Newsletter Stories** from the CD-ROM that came with this book.

2. Press [CTRL][A] (Windows) [⌘][A] (Macintosh) or choose **Select All** from the **Edit** menu to select the entire document.

3. Press [CTRL][C] (Windows) [⌘][C] (Macintosh) or choose **Copy** from the **Edit** menu.

4. Choose **Newsletter** from the **Window** menu (the newsletter you just saved).

5. **Click the mouse in the top of the first column**. Press [CTRL][V] (Windows) [⌘][V] (Macintosh) or choose **Paste** from the **Edit** menu.

Formatting the Headings

1. Select the first heading, **It's Back to School Time** and **boldface** the text.

2. Press [SHIFT][CTRL][>] (Windows) [SHIFT][⌘][>] (Macintosh) to increase the text size to **16**.

3. Make every heading **boldfaced** and **16 point**.

Inserting Clip Art

1. Choose a **clip art** picture to enhance the **first story**. **Note**: See page 82 for help on inserting Clip Art.

2. Choose **Tight** as the text wrap option from **Format Picture**.

Inserting a Watermark

1. Insert a clip art picture into the **Grading Scale** story.

2. Choose **Order**, then **Send Behind Text** from the **Draw** menu [Draw ▾].

3. Choose **Picture** from the **Format** menu. Click the **Picture** tab and choose **Watermark** in **Picture**. See the result on the next page.

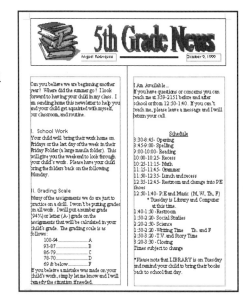

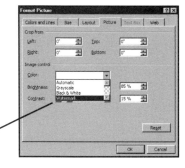

Inserting a Border

1. Select the text at bottom of the Schedule reminding parents to **send library books to school** on Tuesday.

2. Using any method you've learned, **decrease the font size** until it all fits on two lines. This will draw the eye to the paragraph.

3. Select all the text in the **schedule**.

4. Choose **Borders and Shading** from the **Format** menu.

5. Make sure you are in the **Borders** tab.

6. Choose **Shadow** from the **Setting** choices.

7. Choose **4 1/2 pt.** from the **Width** menu.

8. Click **OK**.

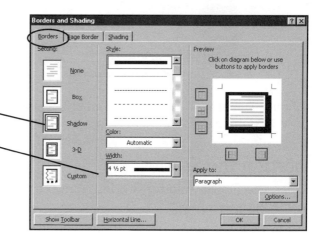

Saving This Issue

1. You're all done! **Save** the file with a name that identifies it as the newsletter with the date so you can find it next month or next year, e.g., Oct 9 News.

Printing This Issue

1. Press CTRL P (Windows) ⌘ P (Macintosh) or choose **Print** from the **File** menu.

The text box lines won't show on the printed newsletter.

Create a Brochure

Create a Great-Looking Informational Brochure

Brochures draw the eye. When we see a brochure, we automatically pick it up and look at it. That's why they are such a good idea in education. Teachers can use the brochure format to present information in a new way to grab kids' attention. Assigning a brochure as a report will allow students to show creativity, as well as what they have learned.

> ### This Activity Covers the Following Topics
> * Setting Up the Page
> * Setting the Columns
> * Viewing the Text Boundaries
> * Inserting a Page Break
> * Understanding the Brochure Layout
> * Creating the Cover
> * Inserting a Text Box
> * Inserting a Picture from a File
> * Creating the Folded-to-the-Inside Page
> * Creating the Back
> * Creating the Inside Page
> * Saving the File
> * Printing the File

Setting Up the Page

Windows

Brochures have very small margins and are frequently laid out on a horizontal page.

1. Create a new *Word* document.

2. Choose **Page Setup** from the **File** menu.

3. Type ".5" for each margin.

4. Click the **Page Size** tab.

5. Click in the **Landscape** radio button. Click **OK**.

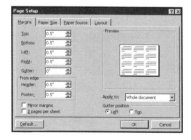
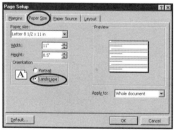

Macintosh

1. Create a new *Word* document.

2. Choose **Document** from the **Format** menu.

3. Type ".5" for each margin.

4. Click the **Page Setup** button.

5. Click the **Landscape** icon next to **Orientation**.

6. Click **OK**, then **OK** again.

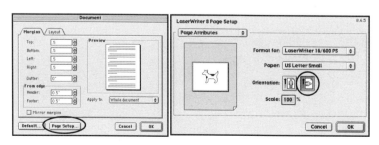

Setting the Columns

Click the **Columns** button ▦ and drag to choose **3 Columns**. **Note:** More information on setting columns can be found in the previous activity.

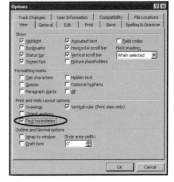

Viewing the Text Boundaries (Optional)

The default for *Word* is for the boundaries to be hidden, but you may find it helpful to see the column boundaries as you are working.

1. Choose **Options** (**Preferences** in versions 98 & 97) from the **Tools** menu.

2. Click **Text Boundaries** and click **OK**.

Inserting a Page Break

1. Choose **Break** from the **Insert** menu.

2. Choose **Page Break** and click **OK**. Now you have two pages with three columns on each.

Understanding the Brochure Layout

One of the most confusing things about creating a brochure is understanding where everything goes. Below is a template for a typical two-page brochure. The outside must have three separate columns of information. On the inside, however, the data can cover one, two, or three columns.

All text in this activity will be graphic text—you'll be able to click and drag it to a new location with the arrow tool. The columns in the document will be used as guides; text will not be typed directly into them. Instead, WordArt and Text Boxes will be created.

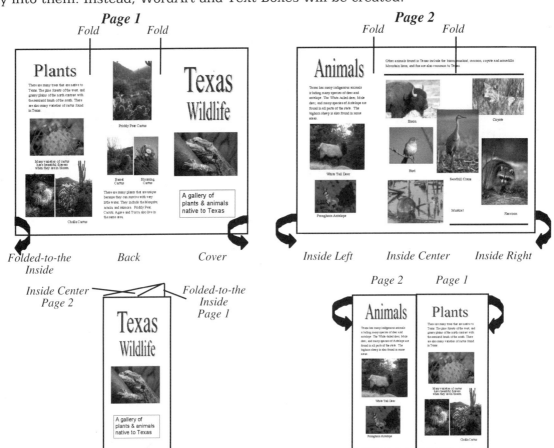

Creating the Cover

1. Click the **WordArt** icon ◢ and choose a style from the gallery.

2. Type "**Texas**" and click **OK**. Move the word to the front cover using the text boundaries to guide you.

3. Click the **AutoText** button again. Pick the same style, and type "**Wildlife.**" Move it under the word "Texas."

Inserting a Text Box

1. Click the **Text Box** icon 🖹 or choose **Text Box** from the **Insert** menu.

2. Drag to draw a text box in the lower left corner of the cover and type "**A gallery of plants & animals native to Texas.**"

3. Choose a **font** and **font size** to contrast with the WordArt text.

Inserting a Picture from a File

1. Choose **Picture** then **From File** from the **Insert** menu.

2. Navigate to the **Pictures** folder on the CD-ROM that came with this book. Double-click a picture of a plant or animal from Texas.

You may need to search the Internet to find other pictures of plants and animals native to Texas (like the armadillo and roadrunner). See page 64 for help.

Creating the Folded-to-the-Inside Page

1. Make a WordArt title called "**Plants**" and place it on the panel that will be folded to the inside.

2. Draw a **Text Box** and write text about the trees of Texas. Sample text might read "**There are many trees that are native to Texas. The pine forests of the west, and grassy plains of the north contrast with the semiarid brush of the south. There are also many varieties of cactus found in Texas.**"

3. Insert pictures of plants from Texas and **create text boxes** to label them.

Creating the Back

The folded-to-the-inside panel and the back panel will both show when the brochure is folded flat, so they may coordinate as in the example above, or the back may be a completely separate panel.

1. Insert a **Text Box describing the plants** native to Texas.

2. Insert **pictures** and **text boxes to label them.**

If you don't want a line around the text box, it's easy to remove. Double-click inside the box and choose No Line from the Line Width box.

Creating the Inside Page

Because the first panel of the previous page will be folded over the center and right panels of this page, it is important to create the left panel to coordinate with that page.

1. **Scroll down** to **page 2.**

2. Make a **WordArt** title reading "**Animals**" and place it on the left panel.

3. Draw a **Text Box** and write text about the animals of Texas and insert pictures.

4. **Create the rest of the page**. You can make 2 separate panels or spread the information across 2 panels.

5. Let's look at the brochure as it will look when printed by turning off the Text Boundaries. Choose **Options** (**Preferences** in versions 98 & 97) from the **Tools** menu and remove the check mark from the **Text Boundaries** box. Click **OK**.

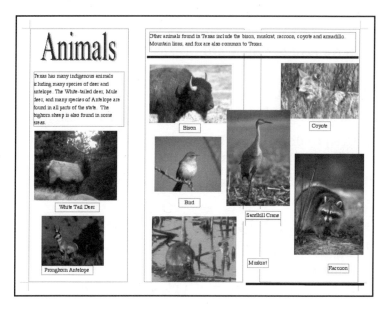

Saving the File

After all this work, you want to be sure to save it! **Save** the file and give it a name you can identify with the project.

Printing the File

1. **Print** the file.

2. Place the **blank sides** of the pages **together** and **fold** the brochure.

3. You may need to change the margins or widen the column guides. Choose **Columns** from the **Format** menu and increase the numbers in the **Spacing** box.

Note: This is just one way to create a brochure. Instead of making all of the text into graphics (WordArt and Text Boxes) you could type as you normally do—directly onto the page instead of using the columns as guides.

Turn to page 134 to see student-created brochures.

Create Linked Pages

Create an Interactive Activity

Most schools allow students to use the Internet for research. To prepare students, teachers can create *Word* files with hypertext that look similar to Internet pages. Students click blue, underlined text (hypertext) to navigate to other *Word* documents to learn about a subject in a controlled environment. When they have opened and read the files created by the teacher, they can open a teacher-created Web page that takes them directly to selected Web sites. You'll learn to link *Word* documents in this activity, then make a related Web page in the next one.

This Activity Covers the Following Topics
- Learning How Hyperlinks Between Files Work
- Creating a Text Hyperlink
- Creating a Graphic Hyperlink
- Learning How Hyperlinks within a Document Work
- Creating a Bookmark
- Creating a Hyperlink within the Document
- Hyperlinking to the Internet
- Using the Internet Link with the Worksheet
- Hyperlinking to *PowerPoint*

Learning How Hyperlinks Between Files Work

1. Open the file "Animals" on the CD-ROM that came with this book.

2. Move the cursor on top of the word "**Mammals**." The word is blue and underlined to indicate that it is linked. Notice that the cursor changes to a hand.

3. **Click** the mouse button. The file "**Mammals**" opens because it was linked to the "Animals" file.

4. Move the cursor on top of the **arrow** at the **bottom of the page**.

   Notice the cursor changes to a hand to indicate that it is linked.

5. **Click** the mouse button. The file "Animals" appears. Notice that the word "Mammals" is now purple to indicate that you have opened that link (just like on a Web page).

6. Click the word **"Rodents"** and then click the **arrow at the bottom** of the "Rodents" page to return to the "Mammals" page.

Creating a Text Hyperlink

1. **Select** the word "**Fish**."

2. Click the **Insert Hyperlink** button .

3. Click the top **Select** button (Browse in 97).

4. **Navigate** to the CD-ROM and select the "**Fish**" file.

5. Click **OK**. The text is blue and underlined.

6. Click the word "**Fish**." The file opens.

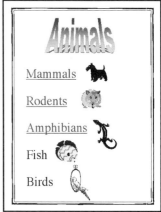

Creating a Graphic Hyperlink

1. **Scroll down** to the **blue arrow** at the bottom of the page.

2. Using the steps in the last section, **link the arrow** to the "**Animals**" file.

3. **Save** the file and then test the link.

4. **Link** the **Birds** file and the **Animals** file.

Learning How Hyperlinks within a Document Work

Hyperlinks and bookmarks work together in lengthy documents to save you time. Instead of scrolling through a long document looking for a certain section, you can set bookmarks and hyperlink to the bookmarks. This allows the reader to jump directly to a section, read it, and then jump back to the top. You've probably experienced this in lengthy Web pages.

1. Open the file "Amphibians Information" from the CD-ROM that came with this book. Notice that the words "Frogs" and "Top" are hyperlinked.

2. Click the hyperlinked word "**Frogs**" in the **first paragraph**.

3. Click the word "**Top**."

Creating a Bookmark

1. **Scroll** down to **page 2**.

2. Select the large word "**Toad**" at the top of the page.

3. Choose **Bookmark** from the **Insert** menu.

4. Type "**Toad**" and click **Add**.

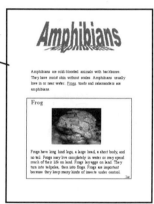

Creating a Hyperlink within the Document

1. Scroll to **page 1**. Select the word "**toads**" in the first paragraph.

2. Click the **Insert Hyperlink** button 📖.

3. Click the bottom **Select** button.

4. Double-click "**Toad**," then click **OK**.

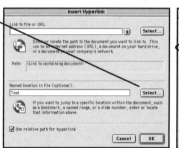

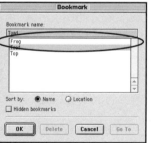

5. **Click the newly linked word "toads"** in the first paragraph. The Toad story appears.

6. Using this method, link the word "**Top**." The bookmark for Top has been created for you.

7. Link the **Salamander** information.

Hyperlinking to the Internet

Students have limited computer time, so when you assign them to do research on the Internet, they can't waste time surfing. Using the hyperlink option in *Word,* you can create a worksheet that includes Web sites you have already researched. Students click on the link and *Word* opens the browser to the chosen site.

1. Open the file "Inventors" from the CD-ROM that came with this book.

2. Click the **Biography.com** icon.

3. Choose **Insert Hyperlink** from the **Insert** menu.

4. Type "**http://biography.com/**".

5. Click **OK**.

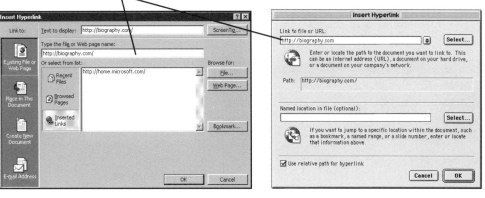

Using the Internet Link with the Worksheet

1. Click the newly created **link**. Your Web browser will launch and go to the Biography.com homepage.

2. Type "**Alexander Graham Bell**" in the search box and press **ENTER** (Windows) **RETURN** (Macintosh) or click **Find**.

3. Read the biography of Bell. When you discover what he invented, go back to *Word* to type the answer.

   Windows users click "**Inventors**" in the **Taskbar** at the bottom of the screen.

Macintosh users choose **Microsoft** *Word* from the **Application Icon** in the upper right corner of the menu bar.

4. Type the answer in the blank area under Alexander Graham Bell.

5. Using the **Taskbar** (Windows) or the **Application Icon** (Macintosh) to move between your browser and the Inventors file, answer the rest of the questions.

Hyperlinking to *PowerPoint*

1. Open the file "Balanced Diet" from the CD-ROM that came with this book. This file is the beginning of a worksheet that is being created to use with students.

2. Drag to select the words "**Food Pyramid Guide**" in the last sentence. You're going to link this to the *PowerPoint* file "Eat Right."

3. Choose **Insert Hyperlink** from the **Insert** menu.

4. Click the top **Select** button (Browse in 97).

5. **Navigate** to the CD-ROM and select the "**Eat Right**" file from the Learning *Word* folder.

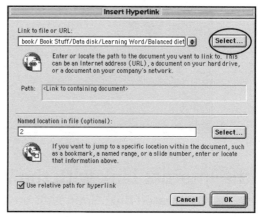

A Balanced Diet

It is very important to have a balanced diet. This means you need to make sure you eat fruit and vegetables; dairy products like milk, cheese and yogurt; carbohydrates like bread, cereal, rice and pasta; meat, including poultry, and fish, eggs, nuts; and fats including butter and oil.

You can see how many servings of each type of food you need by looking at the Food Pyramid Guide.

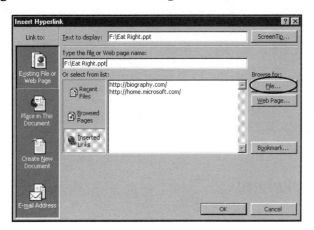

6. Click **OK**. The text becomes blue and underlined.

7. Type "**2**" in the **Named location in file (optional)** box to indicate you want students to look at the second slide in the presentation.

8. Click **OK**. The text will be underlined and blue in color to indicate it has been linked.

Food Pyramid Guide.

9. Click the **linked text**. In versions 98 and 97, the *PowerPoint* program opens to the second slide of the "Food Pyramid" presentation showing the Food Pyramid. In version 2000, click the mouse button to see the second slide.

10. Students will return to the "Nutrition" worksheet for further reading. Windows users click "**Nutrition**" in the **Taskbar** at the bottom of the screen. Macintosh users choose **Microsoft** *Word* from the **Application Icon** in the upper right corner of the menu bar.

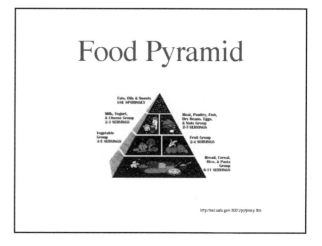

Food Pyramid

Create a Web Page

Create an Animals Web Page

Hopefully, you have learned to create hyperlinked pages from the previous activity. Now you're ready to create a related Web page. Since the linked pages taught the students about animals, this Web page will take the students to good zoo sites so they can learn more about animals. *Word* 2000 has a much improved Web page interface. Virtually anything you create in *Word* will look the same on the Web. Earlier versions will take a few other steps.

> ### This Activity Covers the Following Topics
> - Creating the Title for the Page
> - Inserting Pictures
> - Adding Text to the Page
> - Creating a Table for the Web Sites
> - Formatting the Table
> - Entering the Web Addresses
> - Adding Lines for Interest
> - Saving the File
> - Saving as HTML
> - Viewing the Page as a Web Page

Creating the Title for the Page

1. Create a new *Word* document.

2. Create a **WordArt** title for your Web page. WordArt won't show in your browser if you are creating this page in a version of *Word* other than 2000. If you are using an earlier version, type the title into the document. Use a great color, a large size, and boldface.

3. **Move the title to the center or left side of the page.** (Use the alignment buttons if you are using a version earlier than 2000.)

Inserting Pictures

1. Choose **16** from the **Font Size** menu and a black color if you have changed it.

2. Press ⌨ (Windows) ⌨ (Macintosh) until the **cursor is blinking 2 lines below the title.** If the WordArt moves down, too, just click and drag it back up.

3. Choose **Picture**, then **From file** from the **Insert** menu.

4. Navigate to the **Pictures** folder on the CD-ROM that came with this book. Double-click the **Pictures** folder, then **Animals** and the **Zoo** folder, then on a picture.

5. **Drag** a handle **to make the picture smaller.**

6. **Insert another picture.** (See the example on the next page.)

Adding Text to the Page

1. **Press** ⌨ (Windows) ⌨ (Macintosh) until the cursor is blinking 2 lines below the pictures.

2. Type "**Both wild and domesticated animals live in captivity in a zoo. The keeping of wild animals in captivity began in ancient times. As wild populations continue to shrink in their dwindling habitats, zoos must now fill the roles of breeding grounds and reservoirs of genetic diversity for the many species in danger of becoming extinct. Sometimes there are larger populations of some endangered species in zoos than in the wild. Visit the famous zoos below and check out the animals."**

Creating a Table for the Web Sites

Data on the Web is frequently presented in a table format, especially if it is lined up. You'll be entering Web site names and addresses in a table format.

1. **Press** [ENTER] (Windows) [RETURN] (Macintosh) until the cursor is **blinking 2 lines below the text**.

2. Choose **Draw Table** from the **Table** menu.

3. The cursor turns into a pencil. Drag the pencil diagonally down and to the right to **draw a rectangle.**

4. Drag to **draw a horizontal line across the upper quarter of the rectangle. Draw three more horizontal lines.**

5. Draw a **vertical line in the center of the rectangle.**

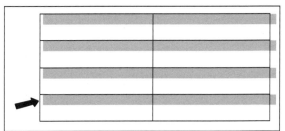

Formatting the Table

1. Click the pencil tool in the **Tables and Borders** toolbar to deselect it.

2. The rows aren't all the same size. Move the cursor to the **first row outside of the table on the left side.** It changes to an arrow. Click and **drag** down to **select all the rows.**

3. Click the **Distribute Rows Evenly** icon. All rows will be the same height.

4. Click the **Text Alignment** arrow and choose **Align Left Center** (Center Vertically in earlier versions) icon to center the text in the row.

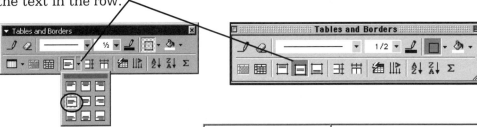

Entering the Web Addresses

1. Click in the upper left cell of the table. Type "**Henry Doorly Zoo.**"

2. Press [TAB] to move to the cell on the right. **Type the Web address.**

3. Press [TAB] and type the next Zoo name. **Fill in the rest of the table.**

Henry Doorly Zoo	http://www.omahazoo.com/
Los Angeles Zoo	http://www.lazoo.org/
Birmingham Zoo	http://www.birminghamzoo.com
Lincoln Park Zoo	http://www.lpzoo.com/menu.html/

Adding Lines for Interest 2000 only

Drawing lines can add interest to a Web page and clearly separate sections of a page. However, the lines won't show in your browser if you are creating this page in a version of *Word* other than 2000. If you are using an earlier version, skip this step and jump to Saving the File.

1. Click the **Straight Line** icon and drag to draw a line between the text and the table.

2. Choose a coordinating color from the **Line Color** icon.

3. Choose a wider line from the **Line Style** icon.

4. Click the finished line and **copy it**.

5. **Paste this line below the table.**

Saving the File

Whenever you create a Web page in *Word*, you need to save it in two ways. You need to save it as a *Word* document and then you need to save it as a Web page.

1. Choose **Save** from the **File** menu.

2. Save the file as you would a *Word* document and name it "**zoopage.**"

Saving as HTML

 2000 only

1. Choose **Save As** from the **File** menu.

2. Choose **Web Page** from the **Save as type** menu.

3. Click **Save.**

4. A warning will appear informing you about the changes that will occur when you save the page. Click **Continue** because you've already saved the page as a *Word* file.

 98 & 97 only

1. Choose **Save As HTML** from the **File** menu.

2. Click **Save.**

3. A warning will appear informing you about the changes that will occur when you save the page. Click **Yes.**

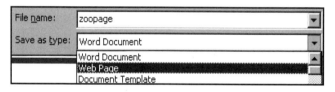

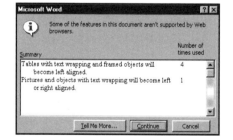

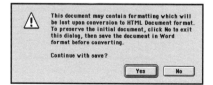

Viewing the Page as a Web Page

1. Click the **Web Layout View** icon or choose **Web Layout** from the **View** menu. In versions before 2000 choose **Web Page Preview** from the **File** menu.

Word 2000 Web Layout

Word 98 Web Page Preview

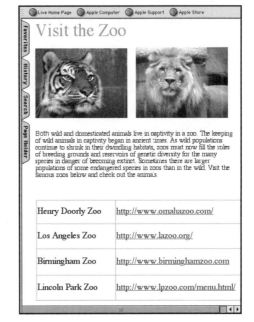

2. Open your browser (Internet Explorer, Netscape Navigator, etc.).

3. Choose **Open file** or **Open** and then navigate to the location where you saved the file as a Web page.

Word 2000 file opened in browser

Word 98 file opened in browser

How Teachers Use *Word*

Detailed Contents

Gary Schlapfer

Friction Lab 105

Simple Machines 106

Light Exam 107

Newton's 3 Laws 108

Temperature Notes 109

Diane Johnson

Moss/Liverwort Lab 110

Great State Lakes Activity 111

Paula Grinvalds

Newsletter 112

Weekly Schedule 113

Joanne Lehman

Class Memory Book 114

Thanksgiving 115

Ruth Follen

Weekly Journal of Snacks for the Week 116

Examining Your School Lunch 117

Body Movement 118

FEEFE Basketball Shooting Assessment 119

"I Can" Basketball Skills Scorecard Assessment 120

Fitness Honor Roll 121

Learning Webs 122

Acrostics 123

Dear Active 124

Personal Goals 125

Multiple Intelligences 126

Lesson Plans 127

Lorna McCloud

How-To Worksheets 128

Diane Wolfe

Vocabulary Bingo 129

Each activity shows pages from its accompanying Word *file.*
The complete Word *files are included on the CD-ROM that comes with this book.*

Notes:

Gary D. Schlapfer

Physics/Space Science

Fremont Middle School

130 East 9th Street

Fremont, Nebraska 68025

402-727-3100

gschlapf@esu2.esu2.k12.ne.us

Physics

Gary uses *Word* to create materials for his classroom because it is so easy and it permits him to create incredible, professional-looking worksheets. Because a picture tells a thousand words, Gary makes liberal use of graphics in his materials, using both clip art and digital pictures he takes of lab experiments. These worksheets make learning Physics both easier and fun!

Friction Lab

Summary

Middle school students perform a physics lab to test the amount of friction caused in various situations. They follow graphic instructions and take notes on printed lab sheets. Experience has taught Gary that today's students are a visual generation. Rather than spending valuable lab time struggling to understand written or verbal instructions, Gary takes digital pictures of lab instructions and incorporates them into the lab worksheet. Instead of telling students to put the weight on the block parallel to the long strip of the sandpaper and pull horizontally, he gives them a picture to follow. "One picture is literally worth all that dialog," says Gary. "Plus it's infinitely more effective. The kids are concerned with getting relevant data, rather than trying to figure out, "How do I set the thing up in the first place?"

Objectives

Middle school students will apply the following skills:

- translate printed and pictured directions into lab operations.
- demonstrate the use of math knowledge to collect, average, and graph data.
- demonstrate cooperative learning skills as the lab is conducted when working with a partner or small group.
- demonstrate the use of higher order thinking skills by applying predictions to novel situations.

Lesson Outline

1. Explain Friction and its application in life and spaceflight.

2. Collect, average, and graph data.

Simple Machines - Inclined Planes

Physics

Summary

Middle school students complete a worksheet to show they can apply concepts they have learned in labs and teaching situations. Gary makes this worksheet graphic because, "I want kids to actually see it and then try and take it to a little bit higher level in Bloom's Taxonomy. They take the information I give them, see it in a novel circumstance, and apply it." In this worksheet they see a drawing of an inclined plane. Then they see it made longer, made shorter, and made taller. Gary asks, "What will that do to your effort?" In the levers section, students identify the effort arm and the load arm, and they are asked, "If you pull down here, what goes up? How do you pull harder? How do the distances compare?" Students then apply these concepts in space.

Objectives

Middle school students will apply the following skills:

- translate printed and pictured directions into lab operations.
- demonstrate the use of math knowledge to complete tasks on the worksheet.
- if working with a partner or small group, demonstrate cooperative learning skills as the lab is conducted.
- verbally explain components of simple machines and their application through an explanation of the lab work conducted.
- demonstrate the use of higher order thinking skills by applying predictions to novel situations.

Lesson Outline

1. Teach inclined planes and levers with concrete examples like teeter-totters; squeezing a kid's hand with your hand, and then with a pair of pliers; discuss bicycles and the gear ratios, the differences where you get force and when you get speed.

2. Assign this worksheet.

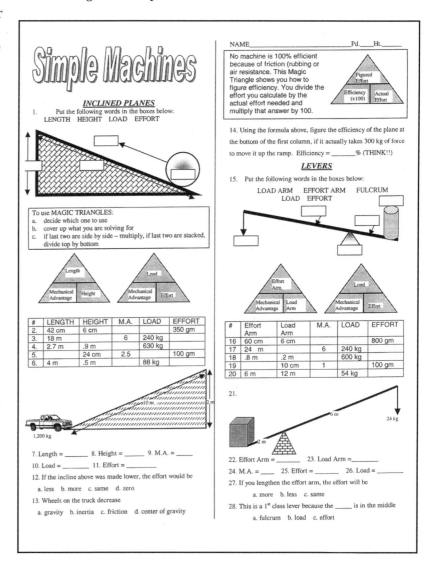

Light Exam

Summary

Middle school students take an exam to show what they have learned about light. The exam is filled with graphic examples of concepts the students have learned during the unit. "The examples are a little bit different from what they saw while learning the unit," says Gary. "It's an open notebook exam. All my tests are open notebook. These exams ask, 'Can you learn it and then apply it on a little bit higher level?'"

Physics

Objectives

Middle school students will apply the following skills:

- translate printed and pictured directions into lab operations.
- successfully complete the assessment on the principles of light.

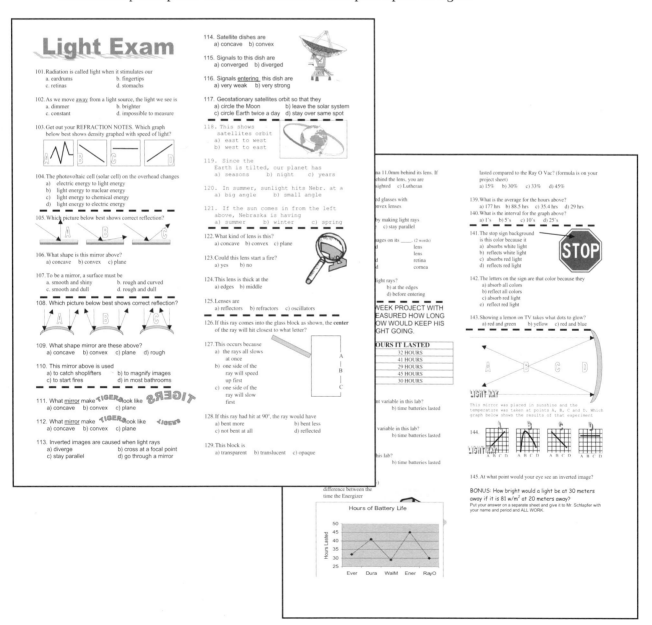

Newton's 3 Laws

Physics

Summary
Middle school students complete a worksheet as they perform lab activities to show they can apply concepts they have learned about Newton's 3 laws in labs and teaching situations. Gary demonstrates these laws through experiments like shooting cans across the room with a firecracker. "They start applying what Newton's laws are visually and verbally, then they do their own experiments which culminates with the Alka-Seltzer Rocket firing up to the ceiling. They easily see how to do it because the digital picture is right in the lab sheet. They snap it in and get out of the way!"

Objectives
Middle school students will apply the following skills:

- translate printed and pictured directions into lab operations.
- demonstrate the use of math knowledge to complete tasks on the worksheet.
- demonstrate cooperative learning skills as the lab is conducted if working with a partner or small group.
- verbally explain Newton's 3 Laws and their application through an explanation of the lab work conducted.
- demonstrate the use of higher order thinking skills by applying predictions to novel situations.

Lesson Outline
1. Teach about Newton and Newton's 3 laws.
2. Demonstrate Newton's laws.
3. Apply the physics of the laws using this lab sheet.
4. Identify variables and constants.
5. More data collection, averaging, and graphing.

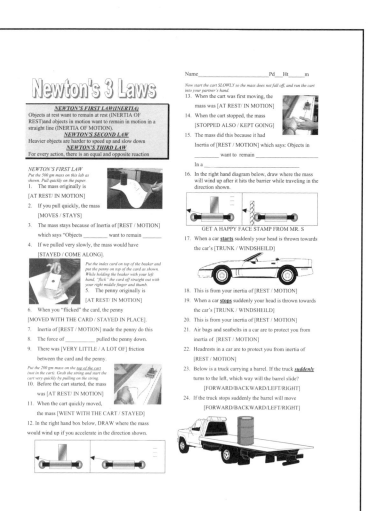

Temperature Notes

Physics

Summary
Middle school students use the Temperature Notes worksheet to take notes during a lecture on the planets. Gary created this worksheet so students can draw pictures, make notes, and write down what makes sense to them as he is teaching.

Objectives
Middle school students will apply the following skills:
- translate verbal lecture into written notes using forms provided.
- demonstrate the use of math knowledge to complete tasks on the worksheet.
- if working with a partner or small group, demonstrate cooperative learning skills as the lab is conducted.
- verbally explain parallel temperature scales.
- draw conclusions about why life can only exist on our planet.
- demonstrate how air pressure effects boiling point.

Lesson Outline
1. Identify parallel temperature scales.
2. Demonstrate "very cold stuff" with dry ice.
3. See why life in this planet is only on this planet.
4. See changes in boiling point with different air pressures.

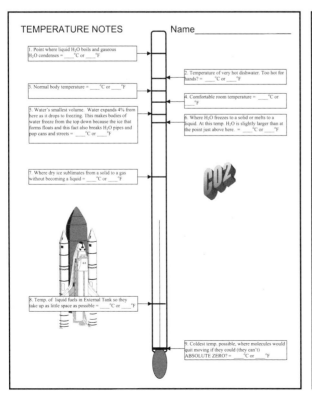

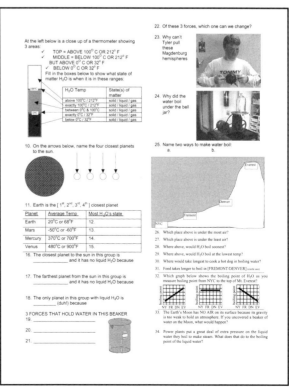

Diane Johnson

Seventh Grade Science Teacher

Fremont Middle School

130 East 9th Street

Fremont, Nebraska 68025

402-727-3100

dlj@etecknetwork.com

Botany

Diane uses *Word* because it is the program that has been chosen by her school. She has her own computer in her classroom and appreciates the ease with which she can create materials to make it easier for her students to complete tasks she wants them to do. Anything she makes in *Word* looks so professional that she's proud to hand it out!

Moss/Liverwort Lab

Summary

Middle school students organize their data on mosses and liverworts while they rotate through lab stations. Students look at the sheet to determine which station to go to, what to do while they're there, where to write their data, and where to draw their observations. Diane says, "This lab sheet helps them stay organized in their data collection. They don't have to try and organize the data on their own, or waste lab time while I tell them where to put their information."

Objectives

Middle school students will apply the following skills:

- translate lab activities into organized written notes using forms provided.
- if working with a partner or small group, demonstrate cooperative learning skills as the lab is conducted.
- verbally describe the physical attributes of moss and liverworts.
- compare and contrast moss and liverworts to other plants.

Lesson Outline

Instruct students about moss and liverworts.

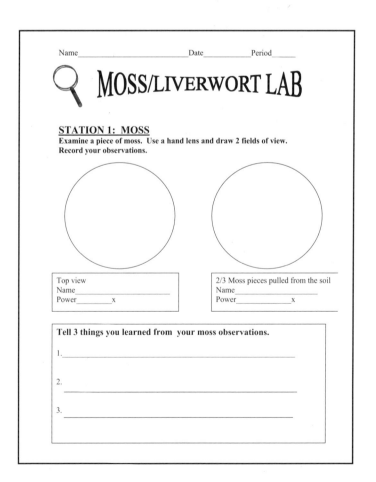

Great State Lakes Activity

Botany

Summary

This activity is a three-part curriculum field trip to Fremont State Lakes. It correlates with the students' unit on plants, leaves, etc. and allows them to apply their knowledge in a practical way. Diane's class made their first field trip in October. One activity was to "adopt" a tree. Students drew a map to their tree and noted wildlife and landmarks around it. In February, students will use their maps to find their tree and repeat the Great State Lakes activity to see changes in the environment, plant life, and wildlife around it. This will be repeated again during Earth Week.

Students work in pairs to fill out the lab sheets. Whenever the teacher blows a whistle, students move to the next activity. The activity includes tree, moss, liverwort, lichen identification, and real-life use of data collection in data tables. Back in class students make a bar graph of the data they collected. Students also make a leaf print T-shirt with leaves they collect and write poetry about the tree they adopted. The rubric is a scoring device to aid students in determining grades and goals of the activity.

Objectives

Middle school students will apply the following skills:

- use of lab sheets to complete "in the field" activities.
- demonstrate the use of math knowledge to complete bar graphs and other tasks.
- work with a partner or small group, demonstrate cooperative learning skills as the activities are conducted.
- demonstrate learning through different modalities including data collection, T-shirt design, and poetry.
- demonstrate the ability to use a rubric to self-assess attainment of activity objectives.

GREAT STATE LAKES ESCAPE
7th Grade Science Activity Requirements

Name:_____
Partner:_____

ACTIVITY 1: ADOPT A TREE

Find a tree that appeals to you and your partner. It can be any type of tree within our exploration area. You will need to collect data about this tree, so pay attention to where you are.

1. MAP THE LOCATION OF YOUR TREE- draw a map below indicating the location of your tree from the bus. Fill in any blanks with your data.

# of paces from bus_____

Direction from bus_____

Landmarks on your way to your tree: (list below)

2. Using your Tree Identification Pamphlet, determine what type of tree you have adopted. Write its name here _____

3. Calculate the height of your tree. Our tree is _____ m.

4. Calculate the diameter of your tree at breast height (DBH). Measure 137 cm above the ground. Our tree's DBH is _____ cm.

NAME_____ DATE_____ PERIOD____

GREAT STATE LAKES ESCAPE RUBRIC

ACTIVITY	TOTAL POINTS	YOURS
1. ACTIVITY 1-ADOPT A TREE		
***all tasks completed correctly	70	_____
***neatness, effort, time	10	_____
2. ACTIVITY 2-SCAVENGER HUNT		
***all tasks completed correctly	20	_____
***neatness, effort, time	10	_____
3. ACTIVITY 3-ANIMAL DATA TABLE		
***all tasks completed correctly	10	_____
***neatness, effort, time	10	_____
4. SIGNS OF HUMAN PRESENCE		
***all tasks completed correctly	10	_____
***neatness, effort, time	10	_____
TOTAL POINTS	150	_____

Paula Grinvalds

Sixth Grade Teacher

Valley Elementary School

301 South Pine Street

Valley, Nebraska 68064

402-359-2151

pgrinvalds@esu3.org

*Language Arts and School
Community Relations*

Paula uses *Word* for everything she possibly can because, "It's so easy to use! Everything I make looks *so* professional! You can insert any kind of graphic and then turn it into a watermark in two seconds flat. It's simple to make columns or tables or anything you want. As far as I'm concerned, it's just about the perfect word processing program!"

Newsletter

Summary

Paula sends home a newsletter on a regular basis to keep parents informed about what's happening in her classroom. The newsletter is written in three columns with a WordArt title. The sample below has a special watermark in the background. Paula took a picture of her class with a digital camera, inserted it into the newsletter document, turned it into a watermark, and sent it behind the text. As the year progresses, Paula turns the newsletter writing and layout over to her students.

Objectives

Sixth grade students will apply the following skills:

- demonstrate writing and editing skills.
- demonstrate cooperative learning skills as the newsletter is developed when working with a partner or small group.
- demonstrate the ability to conduct interviews and to organize information used in the newsletter.
- demonstrate the ability to develop and adjust newsletter layout.

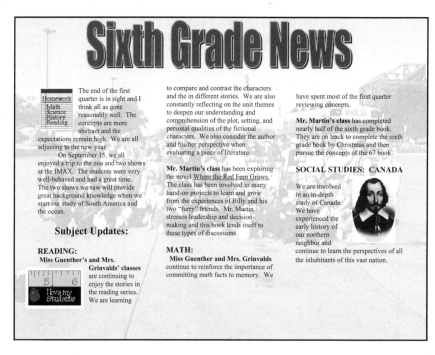

Weekly Schedule

Time Management

Summary

Paula teaches full-time and is the mother of five children, so scheduling is vital to her life. Her family faces the usual issues such as who wants to eat a school lunch and who wants to make his or her own. They also have daily duties like changing out of their school clothes, doing homework, and running several daily paper routes. To make sure everybody gets things done, Paula makes a schedule on Saturday, including dinner menus so somebody can go grocery shopping. She also uses this schedule template to organize herself at school.

This template has a landscape orientation, a WordArt title, and is made up of text boxes. A blank template of this schedule is also included on the CD-ROM that came with this book.

Objectives

- develop a personal weekly schedule using Paula's schedule as a model.
- develop a professional weekly schedule using Paula's schedule as a model.

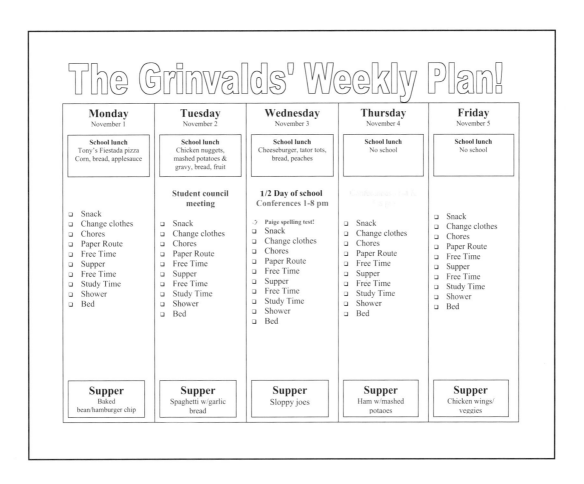

Joanne Lehman

Fifth Grade Teacher

Clarkson Elementary School

1005 N. Clarkson

Fremont, Nebraska 68025

402-727-3178

jlehman@esu2.esu2.k12.ne.us

School Community Relations

Joanne uses *Word* because it's quick and fun to use. "You know how sometimes you get in a rut so you try some new and different things? Then your kids get excited and so do you? *Word* lets me do that," Joanne says. Also her kids have no problem using *Word*; they love it!

Class Memory Book

Summary

Joanne takes digital pictures of her students throughout the year while they perform their daily work. She also takes pictures of their special activities and events. These pictures are inserted into *Word* documents, then bound into a "yearbook" that is given to each student at the end of the year. These "yearbooks" will be especially meaningful since this is the last year Joanne's kids will be in their neighborhood school.

Objectives

Fifth grade students will apply the following skills:

- use keyboarding skills by typing curriculum-related papers.
- use *Word* techniques in writing, such as assigning the use of red for verbs and blue for subjects (or single-underline for verbs and double-underline for subjects).

Favorite Things Joanne Does With *Word*

1. Mail merge for her beginning-of-the-year letter and holiday greetings.

2. Use tables to make her schedules.

3. Use the Comment function to give feedback on student writing projects instead of handwriting comments.

4. Use Format Painter when writing papers to facilitate formatting.

5. Use columns and WordArt to enhance weekly newsletters.

6. Insert clip art from www.hoxie.org/clipart.htm or www.geocities.com/Heartland/Meadows/7597.

Carnival Time

Favorite Things Joanne's Students Do With *Word*

1. Reinforce keyboarding skills by typing curriculum-related papers.

2. Learn new *Word* techniques as they practice keyboarding.

Thanksgiving

School Community Relations

Summary

Thanksgiving is a very special holiday in the United States that inspires people to think about their blessings and appreciate their lives and families. "I truly appreciate the opportunity to work with so many wonderful children, to get to know them and their families," Joanne says, "So I send them a letter every Thanksgiving to say thanks. Using the merge option in *Word* lets me make each letter a personal one."

Objectives

- utilize *Word* and its mail merge function to provide positive communication between school and home to keep parents informed.
- encourage student performance through recognition with parents.

Greetings to the «LastName» Family,

I am so thankful to you for sharing your child, «Child», with me this year. We have had a wonderful year here at Clarkson. Thanks for your help and co-operation, Mr. and Mrs. «LastName», whenever I've needed assistance and support. I am hoping you enjoy this break with your family at «Address1».

«Child», be sure to eat plenty of turkey, enjoy the football games and parades, and be ready to work hard when you return.

This is such a busy time of year Mr. and Mrs. «LastName». Please continue to encourage «Child» to do his best. Again, thank you!

Mrs. Lehman

Ruth Follen

Physical Education Teacher

Fremont Elementary Schools

957 N. Pierce St.

Fremont, Nebraska 68025

402-727-3000

Nutrition

"It's hard to think of teaching before the use of computers to plan, organize, and now interact with students. *Word* has helped add to lessons in creative ways. This in no way takes the place of a creative or inspirational teacher. Computers don't come up with ideas, strategies, or plans for you. But they sure make a lot of ideas come to life for you and your students. *Word* has expanded lessons allowing for more information and learning processes to be used."

Weekly Journal of Snacks for the Week

Summary

Students are assigned to keep track of snacks they eat for a week, "so they know what they're putting in their mouth." They bring the journals back to class and analyze their eating habits.

Objectives

Elementary students will apply the following skills:

- use of snack journal sheet to track eating habits.
- use of higher order thinking skills to analyze eating habits.

5-A-DAY
EAT THE HEALTHY WAY

EATING HEALTHY IS NOT MAGIC

WEEKLY JOURNAL OF SNACKS FOR THE WEEK

1. _____	1. _____	1. _____	1. _____	1. _____
2. _____	2. _____	2. _____	2. _____	2. _____
3. _____	3. _____	3. _____	3. _____	3. _____
4. _____	4. _____	4. _____	4. _____	4. _____
5. _____	5. _____	5. _____	5. _____	5. _____

HOW WOULD YOU JUDGE YOUR SNACKING HABITS?

HOW CAN YOU IMPROVE YOUR SNACKS TO MAKE THEM HEALTHIER?

Examining Your School Lunch

Nutrition

Summary

Students fill in the foods they ate for lunch on a *Word*-created pyramid form that resembles the USDA Food Pyramid. Students determine which food group each food fits into and write it on the line representing that food group on the USDA Food Pyramid. When each food has been listed, students analyze their lunch and decide if they ate a balanced meal.

Objectives

Elementary school students will apply the following skills:

- demonstrate knowledge of the USDA Food Pyramid.
- use higher order thinking skills to analyze individual lunch items.
- categorize food items into the USDA Food Pyramid.
- if working with a partner or small group, demonstrate use of cooperative learning skills.

Body Movement

Summary

Elementary students use the "Body Movement Individualized Program" check sheet to guide them through a gymnastics unit. Ruth calls the unit "Body Movement" rather than "Gymnastics" to keep confusion to a minimum for students who take gymnastics. She begins this unit with second graders. They advance as far as they can given the time constraints and their individual skill levels. Ruth gives students instruction booklets so they can work individually. "I'm trying to instill some 'I'm-not-going-to-spoonfeed-you' techniques. Students can look it up, talk to a partner, and work on a skill. I spend my time going around the mats seeing how they're doing and checking them off." When students complete Level A, they put a sticker on their chart and then start on B. As a result, a class will have some students working on Level A while others are on Level B or Level C. Ruth keeps records so students can follow their progress throughout their elementary years. This way they don't have to repeat any skill levels. If a student is stuck on a skill, Ruth may give that student permission to keep working on that skill while moving on to another.

Physical Education

When students reach certain levels, e.g., Level D, they create a mat routine demonstrating skills learned in previous levels. They list the order of movements, memorize the routine, and perform it for Ruth in the order listed. This allows students to work on memory and to visualize the routine. At the end of the year students create free routines. "I give them some standards, such as you have to do at least 8 moves, showing me some high and some low and a change of direction. Then they have the freedom to make up their own routines and perform them in front of the class. A lot of time kids need that extra work of getting up in front of the class."

Objectives

Elementary students will apply the following skills:

- demonstrate the use of the Body Movement sheet to personalize their Body Movement unit.

- use of self-assessment and evaluation to move through the unit.

- use higher order thinking skills to create a presentation routine.

- if working with a partner or small group, demonstrate use of cooperative learning skills.

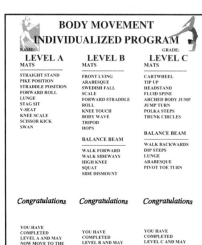

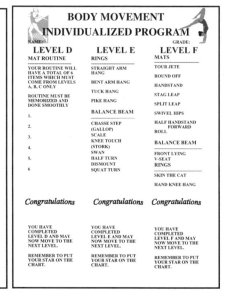

FEEFE Basketball Shooting Assessment

Summary
Elementary students fill out the "FEEFE Basketball Shooting Assessment (Feet, Eyes, Elbow, Flick, Everytime)" check sheet as they practice shooting baskets. To set up for the assessment, Ruth uses three stationary baskets (A, B, C on the sheet) and wheels in a freestanding basket for the center position. Rubber "throw-down" spots mark positions around the floor.

Physical Education

Students run to an empty position and begin shooting baskets while practicing correct form. When a student makes two baskets at a position, he/she fills in the circle on the assessment sheet to indicate success. Students can try as many times as they want from a position to make the baskets. "Nobody's pressuring them," Ruth says, "I'm walking around watching them and offering suggestions. The other kids aren't watching them because they're working on their own thing. They carry around their own paper and pencil, and they do their own marking. Once they've done the close shots, they go back and do the shots at the same basket from a little farther back."

At the end of class Ruth looks at the sheets to determine trouble spots. "We talk about how shooting from an angle is tougher than shooting straight-on, how the backboard helps, and how the farther ones are tougher than the closer ones."

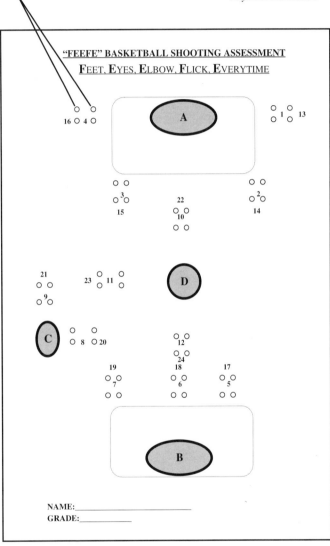

Objectives
Elementary students will apply the following skills:

- practice and improve basketball shooting skills.
- demonstrate the use of the worksheet to track shooting progress.
- use information collected on sheet along with teacher to assess progress.
- if working with a partner or small group, demonstrate use of cooperative learning skills.

"I Can" Basketball Skills Scorecard Assessment

Summary

Elementary students use the "I Can" Basketball Skills Scorecard Assessment sheet to record individual basketball skills. Some of the skills are self-scored, some require a partner. "They're working on shooting, passing, dribbling, timing each other with stopwatches," says Ruth. "They're helping each other, counting for each other, and analyzing each other." It starts out very simple with individual skills, then it gets harder and requires a partner. It's a great way to work on social skills in a fun situation. Students have to take the initiative to go up to someone and say, 'Will you do this with me?' It doesn't have to be the same person each time. This activity gives me a total overview of how they're doing in basketball."

Physical Education

Objectives

Elementary students will apply the following skills:

- demonstrate basketball skills.
- use assessment and evaluation skills (on the scorecard) to determine success in basketball skills.
- when working with a partner or small group, demonstrate use of cooperative learning skills.
- use several multiple intelligences such as body, word, spatial, logical, intrapersonal, and interpersonal skills

---

"I CAN" BASKETBALL SKILLS SCORECARD ASSESSMENT

NAME:_____ GRADE:_____
WHEN YOU ARE ABLE TO DO THE ACTIVITY, PLEASE FILL IN THE CIRCLE IN FRONT OF THE NUMBER.

○ 1. I CAN DRIBBLE 10 TIMES WITH MY RIGHT HAND.
○ 2. I CAN DRIBBLE 10 TIMES WITH MY LEFT HAND.
○ 3. I CAN DRIBBLE 25 TIMES WITH MY RIGHT HAND.
○ 4. I CAN DRIBBLE 25 TIMES WITH MY LEFT HAND.
○ 5. I CAN DRIBBLE TO THE END OF THE GYM WITH MY RIGHT HAND.
○ 6. I CAN DRIBBLE TO THE END OF THE GYM WITH MY LEFT HAND.
○ 7. I CAN ALTERNATE HANDS (STANDING STILL) 10 TIMES.
○ 8. I CAN ALTERNATE HANDS (STANDING STILL) 25 TIMES.
○ 9. I CAN ALTERNATE HANDS TO THE END OF THE GYM.
○ 10. I CAN DO THE PUNCHING BAG DRIBBLE 10 TIMES.
○ 11. I CAN DO 30 DRIBBLES (IN PLACE) 20 SECONDS.
○ 12. I CAN WALK THE BALL SIDE TO SIDE CHANGING HANDS IN FRONT.
○ 13. I CAN DRIBBLE THE BALL AROUND MY BACK CHANGING HANDS FROM A SITTING POSITION.
○ 14. I CAN DRIBBLE THE BALL AROUND MY BACK CHANGING HANDS FROM A STANDING POSITION.
○ 15. I CAN ROLL THE BALL AROUND MY WAIST 5 TIMES.
○ 16. I CAN ROLL THE BALL AROUND MY NECK, WAIST AND LEGS 2 TIMES EACH.
○ 17. I CAN ROLL THE BALL AROUND MY LEGS ON THE FLOOR IN A FIGURE 8.
○ 18. I CAN DO THE FIGURE 8 AROUND MY LEGS 3 TIMES WITHOUT DROPPING THE BALL.
○ 19. MY PARTNER AND I CAN CHEST PASS TO EACH OTHER 10 TIMES FROM THE TWO LONG LINES.
○ 20. MY PARTNER AND I CAN BOUNCE PASS TO EACH OTHER 10 TIMES FROM THE TWO LONG LINES.
○ 21. MY PARTNER AND I CAN OVERHEAD PASS TO EACH OTHER 10 TIMES FROM THE TWO LONG LINES.
○ 22. MY PARTNER AND I CAN CHEST PASS TO EACH OTHER 25 TIMES FROM THE TWO LONG LINES.
○ 23. MY PARTNER AND I CAN BOUNCE PASS TO EACH OTHER 25 TIMES FROM THE TWO LONG LINES.
○ 24. MY PARTNER AND I CAN OVERHEAD PASS TO EACH OTHER 25 TIMES FROM THE TWO LONG LINES.
○ 25. I CAN CHEST PASS INTO THE WALL FROM THE LINE AND CATCH IT 10 TIMES.
○ 26. I CAN DO THE A,B,C,D,E,E,D,C,B,A WALL PASS WITHOUT A MISTAKE.
○ 27. I CAN DO THE A,B,C,D,E,E,D,C,B,A WALL PASS IN NO MORE THAN 20 SECONDS.
○ 28. I CAN DRIBBLE AROUND 5 CONES AND BACK IN NO MORE THAN 20 SECONDS.
○ 29. I CAN MAKE 1 FREE THROW OUT OF 5 TRIES.
○ 30. I CAN MAKE 3 FREE THROWS OUT OF 5 TRIES.
○ 31. I CAN MAKE 5 BASKETS IN 30 SECONDS.
○ 32. I CAN MAKE 8 BASKETS IN 30 SECONDS.
○ 33. I CAN MAKE 10 BASKETS IN 30 SECONDS.
○ 34. I CAN MAKE A BASKET WITH MY RIGHT HAND.
○ 35. I CAN MAKE A BASKET WITH MY LEFT HAND.
○ 36. I CAN MAKE A JUMP STOP AND THEN PIVOT 1/2 TURN.
○ 37. I CAN DO THE ALTERNATING HAND PRETZEL 5 TIMES WITHOUT DROPPING IT.
○ 38. I CAN DO THE WALKING PRETZEL.
○ 39. I CAN DRIBBLE, STOP, DRIBBLE, AND STOP KEEPING THE BALL IN CONTROL.
○ 40. I CAN MAKE A BASKET FROM EACH OF THE 5 POSITIONS BELOW. (FILL IN CIRCLES)

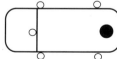

<u>YOU ONLY FAIL WHEN YOU FAIL TO TRY, JUST TRY, TRY YOUR VERY BEST AT ALL TIMES</u>

Fitness Honor Roll

Summary
Elementary students are given the "Fitness Honor Roll" certificate as a reward for working hard and accomplishing their physical fitness goals. Ruth gives out certificates to "pump the kids up" and help them feel good about themselves.

Objectives
Fitness Honor Roll certificate will:

- promote student motivation and the desire to be successful.
- provide recognition for student achievement.

Student Recognition

LET IT BE KNOWN ALL OVER THE
UNITED STATES
THAT THE FOLLOWING
STUDENT OF

GRANT ELEMENTARY
HAS RISEN ABOVE ALL TO
HARNESS THE POWERS OF THE
MIND AND BODY
TO BE PLACED ON THE

FITNESS HONOR ROLL

 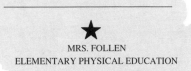

★
MRS. FOLLEN
ELEMENTARY PHYSICAL EDUCATION

DEVELOPING FITNESS IS THE
CORNERSTONE TO TOP PERFORMANCE
AND REQUIRES CONSISTENT,
PROGRESSIVE EFFORT FOR A HEALTHIER
AND MORE ENJOYABLE LIFE .

Learning Webs

Summary

Elementary students map out health-related issues using a web to organize their thoughts. If they are studying fruits and vegetables, Ruth instructs them to write "fruit" in the center oval, then list fruits in the outside shapes. If they are studying smoking, students write "smoking" in the center oval and write effects of smoking in the other shapes.

Objectives

Elementary students will apply the following skills:

- demonstrate use of the "learning web" sheet to organize research.
- demonstrate effective collection of research information for given topics.
- create written report or presentation on the topic.
- if working with a partner or small group, demonstrate use of cooperative learning skills.

Information Collection and Organization

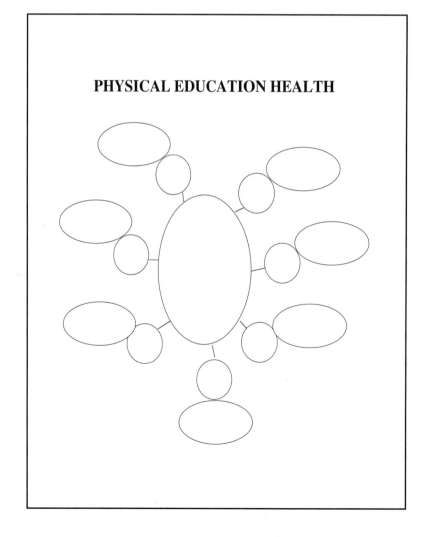

PHYSICAL EDUCATION HEALTH

Acrostics

Nutrition & Language Arts

Summary

Students create Acrostics poetry to show their knowledge of health topics. Once the poem has been created, students create the final copy on the computer using *Word*.

Students write a healthy word vertically, putting each letter on a separate line. Next they write a healthy word or statement that uses the first letter of each line.

Objectives

Elementary students will apply the following skills:

- demonstrate knowledge of health topics.
- use higher order thinking skills to create poems.
- demonstrate use of *Word* to produce the final copy of their poems.
- if working with a partner or small group, demonstrate use of cooperative learning skills.

NAME: GRADE:

PHYSICAL EDUCATION: HEALTH
"APPETIZING ACROSTICS"
HEALTHY POETRY

ACTIVITY:

1. Choose a favorite healthy food. (EXAMPLE - GRAPES)

2. Write the word down the left side of your paper.
(EXAMPLE)
G
R
A
P
E
S

3. Write a healthy word or statement following each of the starting letters. Remember that it must begin with the letter of that it is in line with of the healthy food.

4. Your poetry may be rhyming or free verse.
(EXAMPLE)
Good for you
Running
Aerobics
Pears
Exercise
Strength

5. Be creative with your words or statements for the activity.

6. This project will be done on the computer for your final copy. Make your beginning letter much bigger than the rest of your word or statement.

Dear Active

Summary
Students use "Dear Active" stationery to write a letter to fictional newspaper columnist, "Active," describing healthy dietary and physical activities they have performed during the week.

Objectives
Elementary students will apply the following skills:

Nutrition & Language Arts

- document the recording of weekly dietary and physical activities.
- demonstrate appropriate writing skills.
- use higher order thinking skills in a creative manner to develop letter.

ACTIVE SAYS,

HOW HAVE YOU BEEN ACTIVE THIS WEEK?

DEAR ACTIVE,

I understand that healthy habits are lifetime habits.

Signed _____

Personal Goals

Summary
Before an extended time off from school, e.g., Parent/Teacher conferences or school vacation, Ruth assigns students to decide on a nutritional goal and an activity goal to work on during the break. The goal can be as simple as walking the dog every day, or more intense like running around the block ten times. The nutritional goal can be to eat a particular healthy food or *not* to eat candy. This activity emphasizes the importance of taking home what is learned in school. The assignment is given at least one week before the vacation so students have time to plan. Students tape the completed goal sheet to the side of their desks. During lunch hour, Ruth stops in their room and checks the forms. She signs the sheet if the goals are good and discusses it with the student if more help is needed.

Nutrition & Language Arts

Objectives
Elementary students will apply the following skills:

- demonstrate the use of goal setting for positive effects on lifestyle.
- complete activity which connects home activities with learning activities at school.
- demonstrate connection with Physical Education/Health and lifestyle.

PERSONAL GOALS
FOR _____

PRACTICING HEALTHY LIVING
SKILLS BY SETTING GOALS

1   OCTOBER 28, 29, 30, 31 is when I will work on my goals below :

2   Nutritional goal is : _____

3   Activity goal is :

Multiple Intelligences

Summary

This activity shows how Ruth's Physical Education curriculum breaks down into the multiple intelligences. It helps her analyze the skills she teaches and how they fit into each of the intelligence areas. This analysis helps her meet the needs of each student. Teachers from all content areas can use this model to analyze their own curriculum.

Objectives

- use sheets as an advanced organizer to plan student learning activities using multiple intelligences.
- analyze instructional content by classifying activities against the 8 multiple intelligences.
- demonstrate a linkage between teaching strategies and student learning styles.

Physical Education

HOW ARE THEY
SMART?

BODY
MUSIC
SPATIAL
LOGICAL
LINGUISTIC
INTERPERSONAL
INTRAPERSONAL
NATURE

ELEMENTARY
HEALTH,
WELLNESS AND
PHYSICAL
EDUCATION

RUTH FOLLEN

BODY SMART

<u>HOW CAN I INVOLVE THE WHOLE BODY
OR USE HANDS-ON EXPERIENCES?</u>

⇒DANCING
⇒RUNNING
⇒JUMPING
⇒MOVEMENT
⇒GAMES
⇒FITNESS TESTS
⇒TUMBLING ROUTINES
⇒JUMP ROPE TEAM DRILLS
⇒COOPERATIVE LEARNING
⇒THROWING
⇒CATCHING
⇒STRIKING
⇒CIRCUIT/STATION WORK

Lesson Plans

Summary

Ruth uses the columns and drawing features of *Word* to write her lesson plans. As a traveling Physical Education teacher, Ruth must be organized to ensure that every student is taught the same skills. She creates lesson plans for each skill area in her curriculum.

Objectives

- use sheets developed with *Word* as an advanced organizer to plan student learning activities.
- demonstrate a linkage between teaching strategies, student learning styles, grade levels, and units of instruction.
- create consistency when working with more than one class.

Physical Education

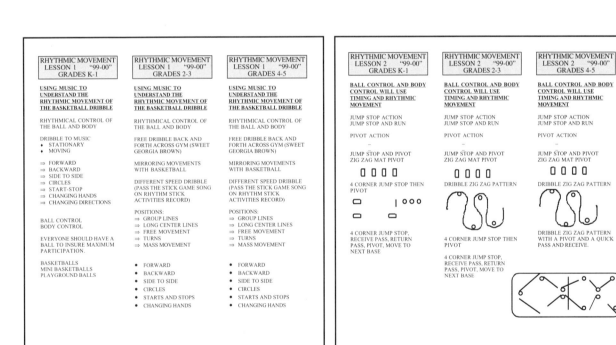

Lorna McCloud

Coordinator of Information & Technology/School Media Specialist

Jackson Elementary School

4340 Edwinstowe Avenue

Colorado Springs, Colorado 80907

719-328-5824

mcclolj@d11.org

Lorna McCloud says, "I use *Word*, *Excel*, *PowerPoint*, and *Outlook* quite often in my job as Coordinator of Info and Tech. I use *Word* whenever I write newsletters to the staff or letters to parents, and I also use it in conjunction with a paint program to create technical documents and directions for my staff. I use *PowerPoint* for presentations, and plan to help my staff train their older students to use it for projects soon. I use *Excel* CONSTANTLY to keep track of purchases, laptop configurations, etc. I haven't learned *Access* yet, but am anxious to do so, and *Outlook* not only keeps me in communication with everyone in the district, its Calendar and Tasks help me keep my world somewhat in order!"

How-To Worksheets

Summary

In her job as technology coordinator, Lorna creates graphic worksheets to help her staff learn to use the myriad of hardware and software available to them. Each teacher in her district received a laptop, so she often does after-school training like this laptop fax one, to help teachers get more use out of their machines. Using *Word*, she creates step-by-step handouts.

Objectives

- demonstrate the use of Microsoft *Office* products for planning and training purposes.

Diane Wolfe

Distance Learning Coordinator/Technology Consultant

Educational Service Unit #2

6320 N. Colorado Avenue

Fremont, Nebraska 68025

402-721-7710

dmwolfe@esu2.esu2.k12.ne.us

As a special education teacher, Diane found that the icons in *Word* made it easy for her kids to use the program. She prefers *Word* because it lets her do everything she wants. "Since most of our businesses are using *Word*, it's important to introduce it to our kids. Kids can easily make the transition from any program or platform, but we should do everything we can to help them. Besides, I just think it's a good product."

All Subjects

Vocabulary Bingo

Summary

Teachers use this Vocabulary Bingo template to create curriculum-based bingo cards for students as a fun way to study vocabulary. Diane recommends just calling the words out the first time so students can match the words on their cards. The second time she recommends reading the definition so kids have to match the word to the definition.

Objectives

Elementary grade students will apply the following skills:

* demonstrate word recognition skills by playing bingo and matching words on card with stated words.

* demonstrate knowledge of word meaning by matching bingo card words with definitions read by teacher.

* if working with a partner or small group, demonstrate cooperative learning skills.

* use *Word* to create their own vocabulary bingo cards.

Vocabulary Bingo
Type Name of Story Here

Use	The	Tab	Key	To
Move	From	Cell	To	Cell
And	Replace	FREE	Each	Word
With	A	Word	From	The
Story	or	Chapter	You're	In

Notes:

How Students Use *Word*

Detailed Contents

Sandi Snyder
Community Brochure Project 133
Technical Writing Assignment 135

Melissa Burns Johnston
Kid of the Month 137
Stories That Grow 138
Tables & Vocabulary 139

Paula Grinvalds
Haiku Poetry 140
My Weekly Plan 141

Joanne Lehman
This is *MY* Locker! 142

Jan Kruse
Primary Publishing 143

Diane Wolfe
My Internet "Bug" Project 144
Christmas Around the World 145
Endangered Animal Research 146
Rainforest Research 147
Science Fair Review 148

Notes:

Sandi Snyder

Computer Teacher

Shickley High School

104 East Murray, Box 137

Shickley, Nebraska 68436

402-627-3375

ssnyder@esu6.esu6.k12.ne.us

School and Community Cooperation

Sandi uses *Word* in her curriculum because Microsoft *Office* is the program her school has chosen to use. She says *Word* is easy to use, is functional and complete, and is user-friendly. Students enjoy using it, and if they need help, they use the online Help built into the program.

Community Brochure Project

Summary

High school students investigate local businesses and create bi-fold, three-column brochures. Sandi says, "This brochure project was designed to make a school-community connection. The first year, students were to create a brochure for a business, organization, activity, etc. in our community. It has since broadened to include businesses in other towns. We wanted our community to see the creativity of our students. The students were given the assignment sheet after our study of Microsoft *Word.* They fold a piece of paper as they would the brochure and then sketch where things will go. This showed that the cover was actually in the third column, minimizing cutting and pasting later. The grading rubric makes it very easy to compile points. Some of the student brochures were actually used by the businesses and organizations."

Objectives

High school students will apply the following skills:

- demonstrate the use of *Word* to create brochures.
- demonstrate cooperative learning skills with other students if working in groups.
- solicit information from area businesses to help in creating the brochure.
- demonstrate the use of higher order thinking skills by creating a new brochure.
- demonstrate the use of time management skills.

Lesson Outline

1. Explain the assignment, including design principles, and show examples of student and commercially created brochures.

2. Allow students to pick their brochure topic and gather information from businesses.

3. Allow students to begin creating the brochures, emphasizing design and time management principles.

Name_____

BROCHURE GRADESHEET

ITEM	POINTS	COMMENTS
Design		
Clip Art		
Word Art		
Spelling/Punctuation/Grammar		
Eye Appeal		

ASSIGNMENT: Tri-fold brochure promoting a business, community, organization, etc.

GRADING: 1. Design example--10 pts--Show a sketch of your brochure to Mrs. Snyder by September 8, 1999 to receive full points.

2. Clip Art--20 pts--Brochure shall include one color clipart AND one picture taken with the Mavica Camera. You may use more.

3. Word Art--20 pts--At least one word art, 2 font styles, 2 font sizes. Use a variety of fonts and positioning to make your brochure attractive.

4. Spelling/Punctuation/Grammar--25 pts--

5. Eye Appeal--25 pts--Adequate use of space, placement of material, info on all 6 panels, etc.

Your brochure CAN include more.

7. Due Date--10 pts--Your final product is due September 22, 1999

Outside of Brochure   *Inside of Brochure*

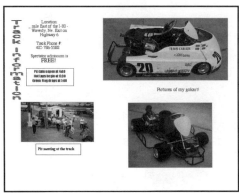

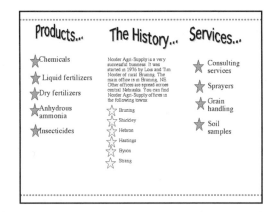

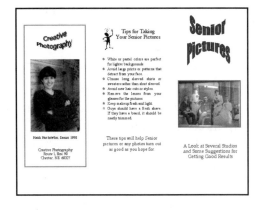

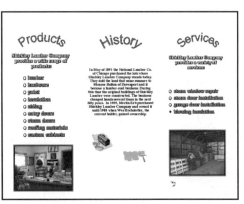

Technical Writing Assignment

Language Arts

Summary

High school students create step-by-step worksheets for students in middle school grades. "After a review of the state standards, this technical writing assignment was created. Technical writing is one skill that businesses feel employees lack. The students create a step-by-step handout geared toward 7th graders to explain one topic from Microsoft *Word*. Some examples: Saving a file, Setting tabs, Creating WordArt, etc. Students use the program *FullShot*, an image capturing software, so they can use parts of the *Word* screen to help clarify the steps." Sandi has a great group of students, and most enjoyed this project. The students knew the grading criteria at the beginning of the project, and the scoring rubric made it easy to compile points.

Objectives

High school students will apply the following skills:

- demonstrate the use of *Word* to create worksheets for middle school students.
- demonstrate the ability to use screen-capturing commands and insert the screen shots in a *Word* document.
- demonstrate cooperative learning with other students if working in a group.
- demonstrate the use of time management skills in completing the project.
- demonstrate their understanding of the grading rubric and activities needed to compile grade points.
- demonstrate the use of technical writing skills.

Lesson Outline

1. Explain the assignment, including design principles, and show examples of student and commercially created technical writing.

2. Allow students to pick their topic.

3. Allow students to begin creating the "how-to" sheets, emphasizing design and time management principles.

Topic	Scoring	Comments
	Needs improvement 5 Average 10 Excellent	
Spelling/Grammar		
Information Correct		
Correct Sequence		
Level of Difficulty		
Incorporation of Visuals		
Peer Evaluation		
Due Date		

You are to construct a handout for the seventh graders. This handout will explain a Microsoft Word topic. The topic is yours to choose, as long as the teacher OKs it! Some ideas would be: How to make a word art, How to select a font and size, etc. Be thorough, complete and use correct grammar and punctuation. Use FullShot to help make your handout clear and easy to understand.

This activity will be due October 6, 1999. Below are the criteria for this activity:

Spelling/Grammar: 20 points
Information Correct: 20 points
Correct Sequence: 10 points
Level of Difficulty: 10 points
Incorporation of Visuals: 20 points
Peer Evaluation: 10 points
Due Date: 10 points

When you want to cut or copy text or pictures from one location and add them to another location there are 2 very simple procedures for doing this, the cut-paste and copy-paste procedures.

Cut-paste: The cut-paste method is used for cutting text or a picture from your document and moving it to a new location within your document. When you cut something, it is saved on the hard drive of your computer. After choosing the new location for your object, you paste it to the new location. Here are the instructions for the cut-paste method.

1. Choose the object(s) you want to cut by highlighting it.

Chelsey Reinsch
(text)

(picture)

2. (A) Cut out your picture or text by either choosing the **Cut** button on the toolbar,

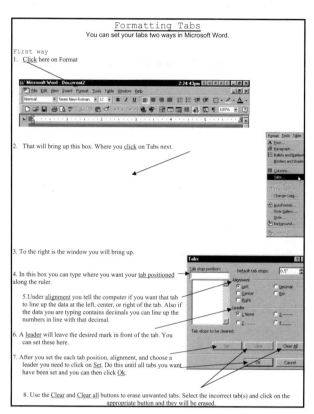

How to Use **WordArt!!!**

1. Microsoft WordArt is a useful tool for creating interesting documents and projects. It lets you color your letters and lots of other cool options. You begin by double clicking on the WordArt icon on the Drawing toolbar, at the bottom of your screen. It looks like this:

2. When you double click on the WordArt icon, it will bring up the WordArt Gallery. The Gallery is the place where you can see all the different styles of letters you can have in WordArt. It looks like this:

3. Look at all your different options! As you can see, you can have letters that are vertical, horizontal, curved, wavy, bright, dark, 3-D, and colored. When you finally decided what kind of letters you want double-click on the box that contains that type of lettering. For example, if I wanted to have 3-D letters, I would double click on this box:

4. Before you go on to the next step of the WordArt process, turn the page of this super-helpful handout to get some more information.

Saving Documents

A very important part of using Microsoft Word is being able to save documents. Sometimes you may need to refer back to a document at a later date, or you may want to finish it another day. Therefore, you want to save the document. Saving allows you to access the file whenever you want.

Steps for Saving Documents:

1. Click on "File" on the menu bar.

2. A dialogue box like this will appear. Click on "Save".

3. This window will appear:

Type in what you want to name the file.

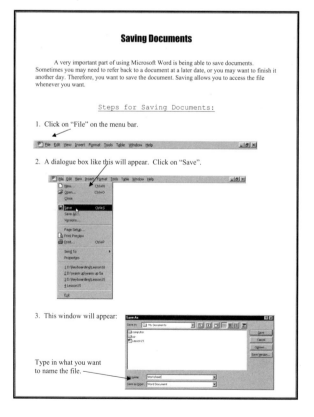

Melissa Burns Johnston

Teacher of Gifted and Talented Students

Anahuac Middle School

706 Mikhaeal Ricks Drive

Anahuac, Texas 77514

409-267-3421

johnstonm@anahuac.isd.esc4.net

Any Subject

Technology has been a vital part of Melissa's gifted and talented classroom for several years. "I knew I had to jump on the technology bandwagon if I was going to keep up with my G/T kids. Technology is their reality, and I wanted to be a part of it! It's a natural fit for the product-based learning that goes on in my Challenge classrooms."

Kid of the Month

Summary

Middle school students generate a personal resume (with teacher-directed guidelines) for their portfolio. Resumes can have a theme like applying for Kid of the Month, Scientist of the Month, Inventor of the Month, etc.

Objectives

Middle school students will apply the following skills:

- demonstrate thinking skills, including analysis to determine what information will be used for "selling" one's self.
- use of word processing skills by completing the appropriate "Kid of the Month" form.
- demonstrate the understanding of *Word*'s Resume Wizard feature to create a resume.

Lesson Outline

1. Explain the assignment and how it fits in the curriculum.

2. Discuss the concept of selling yourself, picking out your best points, defining your skills, deciding what you want people to know about you. Discuss importance of listing extracurricular activities, offices held, community service, etc.

3. Have students put their personal information in the appropriate form. To incorporate word processing, give students the file and allow them to enter their information. Otherwise, duplicate a printed version and allow students to handwrite their information.

4. Demonstrate the Resume Wizard in *Word* to the class. Allow students to create their own resume, incorporating data listed in the previous step.

5. Students or a group of teachers vote on the best resume to choose Kid of the Month. These can be posted on bulletin boards, sent to principals, counselors, etc.

Stories That Grow

Language Arts

Summary
Middle school students in a lab or mini-lab situation begin typing a story in *Word* (this works especially well with Halloween or other holiday stories). The teacher gives them 3-5 minutes. On a signal from the teacher, students move to the next computer. They read what has been written and then continue the story, but they must write in a different color to distinguish what they've written. This writing and moving continues until the story comes around to the original author(s). **Note**: Melissa warns that kids love nothing more than to change the direction the authors intended when they began the story! It adds a whole new, fun element to the activity.

Objectives
Middle school students will apply the following skills:
- demonstrate the use of *Word* to write stories in a lab setting.
- demonstrate cooperative learning with other students.
- demonstrate reading skills and comprehension of previously printed story segments.
- demonstrate the use of time management skills in completing their story section.
- demonstrate use of higher order thinking skills through their creativity in synthesizing new stories.

Lesson Outline
1. Explain the assignment and how it fits into the curriculum.

2. Have students pick a color for their writing.

3. Assign individual students or groups to computers and allow them to begin writing.

4. Print the stories when finished. The stories can be published on the school server or projected to practice editing, revising, and elaboration skills.

Stories That Grow

In this activity you will become authors of own stories that grow and GROW! To get started type the beginning of an original story on any subject you choose. When the teacher calls "time", you are to move to the computer to your right and sit down. Read the story on your screen and when the teacher signals, begin adding to the story. Be sure to type in a different colored font than the previous person. This process will continue until you arrive back at your first seat. Have fun!

TYPE YOUR NAME HERE

Begin writing a super story here!

Tables & Vocabulary

Summary

This activity can be used in any curriculum area. The teacher creates a three-column table and inserts vocabulary words in column one. Students then type related words in the other columns or handwrite the words if the sheet is duplicated.

Objectives

Middle school students will apply the following skills:

Any Subject

- demonstrate the use of *Word* to complete the table of vocabulary words or handwrite the words.
- if working with a partner or small group, demonstrate cooperative learning with other students.
- use analysis skills to identify related words to words provided by the teacher.
- demonstrate the use of time management skills in completing the project.
- demonstrate vocabulary skills.

Lesson Outline

1. Explain the assignment and how it fits into the previously taught curriculum.

2. To incorporate word processing into this phase of the assignment, give students the teacher-created file and allow them to type in their information. Otherwise, duplicate a printed version and allow students to handwrite their information.

DESCRIBE IT!

Choose two adjectives to describe each noun listed. Do not use any adjective more than once.

NOUN	ADJECTIVE #1	ADJECTIVE #2
Sandwich	Delicious	Satisfying
Friend	Faithful	Exciting
Automobile	Convenient	Economical
Book	Intriguing	Lengthy
Summer	Steamy	Free
Crayon	Colorful	Slender
Map	Informative	Reliable
Computer	Advanced	High-tech
Classroom	Educational	Crowded
Park	Shady	Quiet
Mountain	Rocky	Dangerous
Freedom	Unchained	everlasting

TIME MARCHES ON

Choose two adjectives to describe each time period in America in the 20th century. Ask for help from parents, grandparents, and other family members! Use each adjective only once. Good Luck!

DATE	ADJECTIVE #1	ADJECTIVE #2
1900-1909	Tragic	Revolutionary
1910-1919	Musical	Hostile
1920-1929	Glamorous	Depressing
1930-1939	Unemployed	desperate
1940-1949	Catastrophic	Serene
1950-1959	Innovative	Scientific
1960-1969	groovy	Turmoiled
1970-1979	Scandalous	Eventful
1980-1989	Explosive	caring
1990-1999	Technological	Controversial

Table creation is described on page 67.

Paula Grinvalds

Sixth Grade Teacher

Valley Elementary School

301 South Pine Street

Valley, Nebraska 68064

402-359-2151

pgrinvalds@esu3.org

Language Arts

Paula uses *Word* for everything she can. She says, "Kids love to publish their work. If I give them a chance to write their assignments in a word processor, they are much more willing to edit and make changes, so their work is much better."

Haiku Poetry

Summary

Middle school students write haiku poetry, then jazz it up with graphics including watermarks and graphics from the Internet.

Objectives

Middle school students will apply the following skills:

- demonstrate their understanding of haiku structure by writing their own poems.
- demonstrate their use of different features within *Word* by inserting pictures, formatting pictures into watermarks, copying pictures from the Internet and pasting into a *Word* file.
- demonstrate the use of higher order thinking skills by creating their haiku presentation.

Lesson Outline

1. Introduce students to haiku poetry.

2. Demonstrate how to insert pictures into a *Word* file.

3. Demonstrate how to format a picture into a watermark.

4. Demonstrate how to copy and paste or insert an Internet picture into a *Word* file.

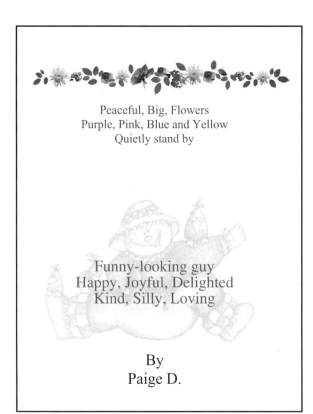

Peaceful, Big, Flowers
Purple, Pink, Blue and Yellow
Quietly stand by

Funny-looking guy
Happy, Joyful, Delighted
Kind, Silly, Loving

By
Paige D.

My Weekly Plan

Summary

Middle school students open the "My Weekly Plan" file and enter their weekly schedule. The WordArt title can be edited to replace the word "My" with the student's name. As an alternative, teachers can print the file, duplicate it, and allow students to handwrite their schedules. As an extension of the activity, students can use the Text Box function in *Word* to create weekly schedules. Depending on their learning style, after they have created a computer-generated schedule, students can update them every week on the computer or handwrite them on duplicated schedule forms.

Time Management

Objectives

Middle school students will apply the following skills:

- using Paula's schedule as a model, develop a personal weekly schedule.
- if working with a partner or small group, demonstrate cooperative learning skills as weekly schedule is developed.
- demonstrate the ability to follow an organized framework.
- demonstrate the use of *Word* features including WordArt, text boxes, and editing features.

Lesson Outline

1. Discuss the principle and value of time management.

2. Demonstrate how to enter schedule data into the schedule.

3. Demonstrate how to edit the WordArt title to include the student's name.

4. As an extension activity, demonstrate how to create text boxes and schedule forms.

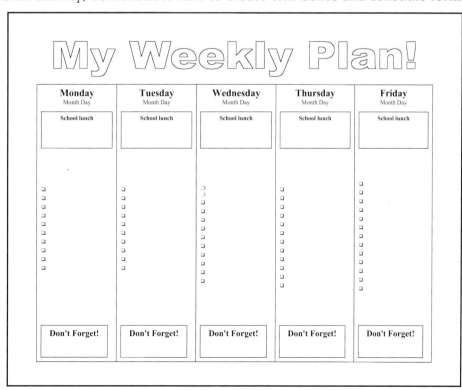

Joanne Lehman

Fifth Grade Teacher

Clarkson Elementary School

1005 N. Clarkson

Fremont, Nebraska 68025

402-727-3178

jlehman@esu2.esu2.k12.ne.us

Art & Design

Since kids are so into technology, it is easy to take advantage of their enthusiasm by incorporating technology into lessons. Kids think they are getting to do cool stuff on the computer (and they are), but at the same time, they are reinforcing key concepts.

This is *MY* Locker!

Summary

Students will use *Word* to create name tags for their lockers. Use of WordArt, page borders, inserting clip art and pictures from the Internet will be emphasized.

Objectives

Middle school students will apply the following skills:

- use of WordArt, including the changing of colors and sizes.
- demonstrate ability to insert clip art and pictures.
- demonstrate ability to copy and download pictures from the Internet.

Lesson Outline

1. Demonstrate WordArt, including how to change size and color.

2. Demonstrate Borders and Shading to make page borders.

3. Demonstrate how to insert clip art and pictures into a *Word* file.

4. Demonstrate how to copy or download pictures from the Internet.

5. Demonstrate how to paste or insert an Internet picture into a *Word* file.

6. Demonstrate how to use Drawing tools.

Jan Kruse

Language Arts

Media Specialist

Fremont Elementary Schools

Fremont Public School District

957 N. Pierce St.

Fremont, Nebraska 68025

402-727-3023

Jan says using *Word* with primary children may seem an unlikely possibility. However, a simple and easy-to-prepare template can provide a publishing opportunity for students as young as those in first grade. It is very helpful if students bring an "edited" document to the computer so they can focus on keyboarding their stories. Illustrations may be done by hand once the story is published or when they can use the draw tools to complete their work.

Primary Publishing

Summary

Students will use *Word* to publish stories. They will use a Drop Cap to make their work look "just like a real picture book," and leave room at the top of the page to draw an illustration by hand or with draw tools.

Objectives

Primary students will apply the following skills:

- demonstrate writing and editing skills.
- demonstrate the use of Drop Caps.
- use *Word* to type stories and create space for illustrations.
- demonstrate art skills by creating illustrations.

Lesson Outline

1. Open the document template (landscape orientation and large type size) or demonstrate the difference in page orientation.

2. Demonstrate pressing ⌷ENTER⌷ (Windows) ⌷RETURN⌷ (Macintosh) to leave blank space at the top of the page for drawing a picture.

3. Demonstrate use of Drop Cap to begin the first page of a story, just like a real picture book.

4. Demonstrate printing setup and sequence of printing.

I went to the zoo. I saw an elephant. It was gray. It had a long nose.

Science

Diane Wolfe

Distance Learning Coordinator/Technology Consultant

Educational Service Unit #2

6320 N. Colorado Avenue

Fremont, Nebraska 68025

402-721-7710

dmwolfe@esu2.esu2.k12.ne.us

As a special education teacher, Diane found that the icons in *Word* made it easy for her kids to use the program. She prefers *Word* because it lets her do everything she wants. "When most of our businesses are using *Word,* it's important to introduce it to our kids. Kids can easily make the transition, but we should do everything we can to help them. Besides, I just think it's a good product."

My Internet "Bug" Project

Summary

First and second grade students use the Internet to study metamorphosis. Students use the worksheet created in *Word* to write a sentence about what they learned about each of the four stages of metamorphosis, using the pictures as a guide.

Objectives

Primary grade students will apply the following skills:

- demonstrate the understanding of the four stages of metamorphosis.
- demonstrate use of the Internet by navigating through a Web site.
- complete the worksheets provided for the "bug" project.

Lesson Outline

1. Teach the four stages of metamorphosis.

2. Bookmark the Web site http://www.geocities.com/Heartland/9379/monarch.html.

3. Go on the Web site and work with students as they go through the site.

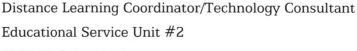
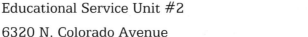
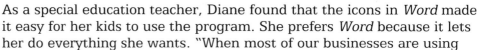
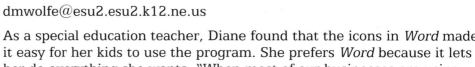

Christmas Around the World

Summary
Students use the Internet to search for Christmas customs from around the world. They color in their country on the map at the bottom of the worksheet and fill in the rest of the information as they research their project.

Multicultural Education

Objectives
Intermediate students will apply the following skills:
- identify various cultural celebrations of Christmas.
- search Web sites to find Christmas celebrations.
- create a "Christmas Around the World" booklet.
- if working with a partner or small group, demonstrate cooperative learning skills.

Lesson Outline
1. Discuss holidays around the world and how they vary.
2. Find good Web sites for students to use in their research.
3. Create a "Christmas Around the World" booklet from everybody's sheets.

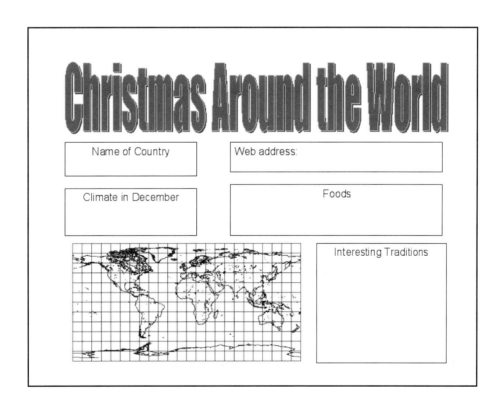

Endangered Animal Research

Ecology

Summary
Students use the Internet to do research about an endangered animal. The worksheets lead students through the research as they find the scientific name of the animal, its habitat, its size, threats to its livelihood, and other information about the animal. Students will also write the Web site address as bibliographic information. Penmanship could also be incorporated.

Objectives
Intermediate students will apply the following skills:
- demonstrate ability to access the Internet and locate assigned Web sites.
- ability to collect information about their endangered animal.
- demonstrate cooperative learning skills if working with a partner or small group.
- demonstrate completion of worksheets for assignment.

Lesson Outline
1. Discuss endangered animals.

2. Find good Web sites for students to use in their research.

3. Assign students to research an animal.

4. Have students complete worksheets.

Endangered Animal Investigation

Name of Animal:

Web Address:

Created by:

Write the name of your animal in cursive:

Important Information

Threats

Scientific Name:

Habitat

Size

Threats

Other Information

Rainforest Research

Ecology

Summary

Students use the Internet to find information about the rainforest's plants and animals. They pick an interesting plant and animal; record where in the rainforest they live; record neat information about them; draw a picture of them; and write what the animal eats. Students also give bibliographic information about the Web site. Reading *The Great Kapok Tree, A Tale of the Amazon Rainforest* by Lynne Cherry incorporates literature into the lesson as well as add to student understanding. Penmanship could also be incorporated.

Objectives

Intermediate students will apply the following skills:

- demonstrate ability to access the Internet and locate appropriate Web sites.
- ability to collect information about their rainforest plant or animal.
- if working with a partner or small group, demonstrate cooperative learning skills.
- demonstrate completion of worksheets for assignment.

Lesson Outline

1. Read *The Great Kapok Tree, A Tale of the Amazon Rainforest* by Lynne Cherry.

2. Discuss the rainforest.

3. Find good Web sites for students to use in their research.

4. Assign students to begin researching the rainforest.

5. Assign students to fill in the information they find.

Rainforest Information

Location of Rainforest:

Web Address:

Created by:

Plant Information

Neat Information

Name:

Other Information

Size

Picture of my plant

Where in the Rainforest does it live?

Animal Information

Neat Information

Name:

What does it eat?

Size

Picture of my animal

Where in the Rainforest does it live?

Science Fair Review

Science

Summary

Students use the Science Fair Peer Review Sheet as a guide to evaluate science fair projects of other students. The focus of this sheet is to have students help each other on science fair projects before they go to the science fair where their projects will be judged. The sheet could be changed to a self-evaluation.

Objectives

Middle school students will apply the following skills:

- use of the "Peer Review Sheet" to access the projects of others.
- use of higher order thinking skills to analyze and evaluate the work of peers.
- demonstrate cooperative learning skills.

Science Fair Peer Review Sheet

Project Title: _____

Student Name(s) _____
_____

School: _____

<u>To Be Completed by Judge:</u>

	Things Done Well	Things to Remember For Next Time
Scientific Thought/Research (planning, expert advice sought, etc.)		
Data Collection (data supports project, enough data, lab notes)		
Creative Ability (original, unique style of displaying info.)		
Presentation to Judges (3-5 minutes, well organized, presenters poised and confident)		
Display (attractive, eye catching, spelling, carefully constructed)		

Additional Comments: _____
_____
_____
_____
_____

Reviewer's signature: _____

Appendix

Detailed Contents

Word Menu Differences 151

Help! I Want to Share My *Word* File 154

Change the RAM (Memory) Allocated to *Word* 156

Animals 158
Amphibians 158
Birds 159
Fish 163
Zoo 164
Mammals 165
Rodents 166
Reptiles 167
Insects 168

Plants 169
Fruit, Berries, and Seeds 169
Flowers 170
Mushrooms 172
Cacti 173

Index 175

Notes:

Word Menu Differences

File   Edit   View   Insert   Format   Tools   Table   Window   Help

File Menu

Word 2000

Word 97

Word 98

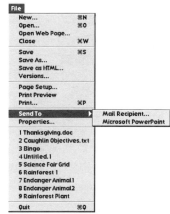

Edit Menu

Word 2000

Word 97

Word 98

Menus aren't always the same in each version. This is especially true for Word 2000. Initially only the most used items appear. Click ⦙ to see all the menu items. If you use hidden items frequently, they will move up and unused ones will move down.

View Menu

Word 2000

Word 97

Word 98

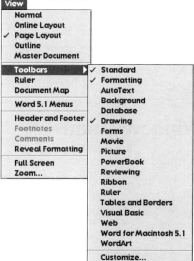

File   Edit   View   Insert   Format   Tools   Table   Window   Help

Insert Menu

Word 2000

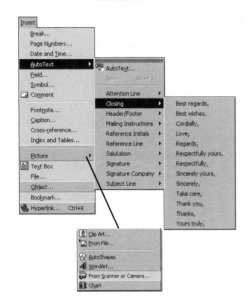

Word 97

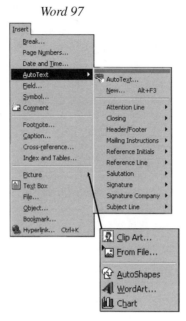

Word 98

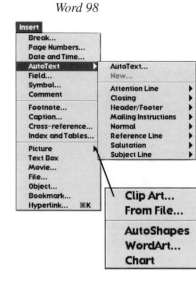

Format Menu

Word 2000

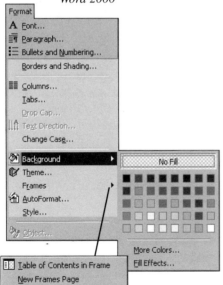

Word 97

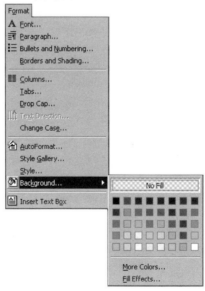

Word 98

Format	
Font...	⌘D
Paragraph...	⌘⌥M
Document...	
Bullets and Numbering...	
Borders and Shading...	
Columns...	
Tabs...	
Drop Cap...	
Text Direction...	
Change Case...	
AutoFormat...	
Style Gallery...	
Style...	
Background	
Insert Text Box	

Window Menu

Word 2000

Word 97

Word 98

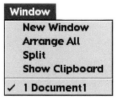

Tools Menu

Word 2000

Word 97

Word 98

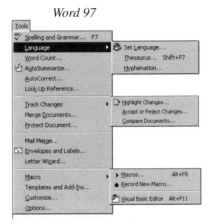

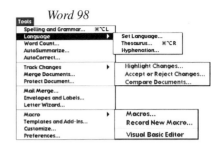

Table Menu

Word 2000

Word 97

Word 98

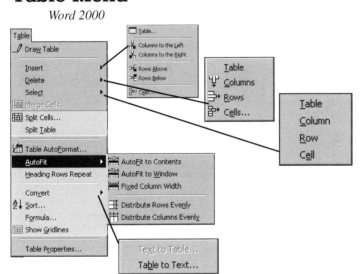

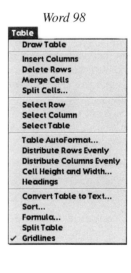

Help Menu

Word 2000

Word 97

Word 98

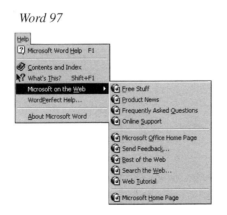

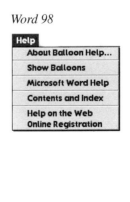

Help! I Want to Share
My *Word* File...

PROBLEM:

1. Recipient Does <u>Not</u> Have *Word*, & Wants to "View Only." In other words, the person with whom you are sharing your *Word* file (the recipient) simply wants to be able to view the file in full and maybe print it. The recipient does <u>not</u> need to be able to edit the file.

2. Recipient Has a Different Version of *Word*, & Wants to Both "View and Edit." In other words, your recipient has *Word* but it is a different version than the one you created the file in or the recipient is running *Word* on a different computer platform (e.g., Macintosh instead of Windows). You want your recipient to be able to view and change your *Word* file with no loss of data.

3. Recipient Uses Something Other Than *Word*, & Wants to View and/or Edit.

SOLUTION:

1. If Recipient Uses Windows, She Only Needs the Free *Word* Viewer.

Good news:

o If your recipient is a **Windows** user and all she wants to do is view the presentation (i.e., she will not need to edit it), then she does not even need to have *Word,* just the **Word Viewer.**

Bad news:

o There is no *Word* Viewer for **Macintosh** users. See solution 2 below if recipient has a Macintosh.

2. Be Careful When Opening Files in Different Versions of *Word*. Things can get a bit more complex here, but there is still reassuring news.

Good news:

o Since version 6.0 came out, *Word* has been a "cross-platform" application. That means that as long as the recipient of your file has the **same version** of *Word* you used, but is just running it on a **different platform** (Macintosh instead of Windows, or vice versa), your file should open, with no loss of original data.

o If the recipient of your file has a **newer version** of *Word* than the one with which you created the file, then again, she can open your file with no loss of data. Note: For versions earlier than 6.0, the recipient would need to open the file at least on the **same platform** (i.e., Windows or Macintosh) on which you created the file.

Bad news:

o In all other situations where the recipient has an **older version** of *Word* there are a few limits on your ability to share the file. First, you will either need to save the file in an older format before sending it, or else the recipient needs to install a "post-ship converter" (see chart on next page). Second, some data from the file created with the newer version of *Word* will be lost when the recipient opens it in an older version.

3. Be Careful When Opening *Word* Files in Different Word Processing Programs. Your Best Bet Is to Save File As "RTF" Instead.

Bad news:

o In situations where the recipient uses a program **other than** *Word,* there are limits on your ability to share a *Word* file. The best way to ensure the file will open with **most formatting intact** is to save the file in **RTF** (Rich Text Format, one of the options in the "Save As" window) before sending the file. More risky alternatives, in terms of the file opening and data being intact, include relying on the recipient's program having the appropriate "converter" to read your *Word* file as is, and saving the file in the format the recipient uses (check the options in the "Save As" window).

Still confused about what happens when you open files in different versions of *Word*? The following page contains an easy-to-use chart to help you sort through compatibility issues.

When File Created With... / Is Opened With... — Word version compatibility chart

Safe Bet	Is Opened With... ↓ / When File Created With... →	MACINTOSH — Word 98/Office 98 (8.0) (Power PC only)	MACINTOSH — Word 6.0	MACINTOSH — Word 5.x	MACINTOSH — Word 4.0	WINDOWS 95/98/NT — Word 2000/Office 2000 (9.0)	WINDOWS 95/98/NT — Word 97/Office 97 (8.0)	WINDOWS 95/98/NT — Word 95/Office 95 (7.0)	WINDOWS — Word 6.0	WINDOWS 3.x — Word 2.0
☞	Word 98/Office 98 (8.0) (Power PC only)	OK	OK	OK	OK	OK	OK	OK	OK	OK
	Word 6.0	OK, if 97-2000 Import Converter installed in 6.0 folder, or if 98 file saved as 6.0 **SOME DATA LOSS***	OK	OK	OK	OK, if 97-2000 Import Converter installed in 6.0 folder, or if '00 file saved as 6.0 **SOME DATA LOSS***	OK, if 97-2000 Import Converter installed in 6.0 folder, or if 97 file saved as 6.0 **SOME DATA LOSS***	OK	OK	OK **SOME DATA LOSS**
	Word 5.x	OK, if 97-2000 Import Converter installed in 5.x folder, or if 98 file saved as 4/5 **SOME DATA LOSS***	OK, if 6.0 Import Converter for 5.x installed in 5.x folder, or if 6.0 file saved as 4/5 **SOME DATA LOSS****	OK	OK	OK, if 97-2000 Import Converter installed in 5.x folder, or if 2000 file saved as 4/5 **SOME DATA LOSS***	OK, if 97-2000 Import Converter installed in 5.x folder, or if 97 file saved as 4/5 **SOME DATA LOSS***	OK, if 6.0 Import Converter for 5.x installed in 5.x folder, or if 7.0 file saved as 4/5 **SOME DATA LOSS****	OK, if 6.0 Import Converter for 5.x installed in 5.x folder, or if 6.0 saved as 4/5 **SOME DATA LOSS****	OK **SOME DATA LOSS**
	Word 4.0	OK, if 98 file saved in 4/5 **SOME DATA LOSS***	OK, if 6.0 file saved in 4/5 **SOME DATA LOSS****	OK	OK	OK, if 2000 file saved as 4/5 **SOME DATA LOSS***	OK, if 97 file saved as 4/5 **SOME DATA LOSS***	OK, if 7.0 file saved as 4/5 **SOME DATA LOSS****	OK, if 6.0 file saved as 4/5 **SOME DATA LOSS****	OK **SOME DATA LOSS**
☞	Word 2000/Office 2000 (9.0)	OK	OK	OK	OK	OK	OK	OK	OK	OK
☞	Word 97/Office 97 (8.0)	OK	OK	OK	OK	OK VIEW ONLY	OK	OK	OK	OK
☞	Word 97-2000 Viewer for Windows 95-98 (free)	OK VIEW ONLY	OK VIEW ONLY	OK VIEW ONLY	OK VIEW ONLY	OK VIEW ONLY	OK VIEW ONLY	OK VIEW ONLY	VIEW ONLY	VIEW ONLY
	Word 95/Office 95 (7.0)	OK, if 97-2000 Import Converter installed in 7.0 folder, or if 98 file saved as 6/7 **SOME DATA LOSS***	OK	OK	OK	OK, if 97-2000 Import Converter installed in 7.0 folder, or if '00 file saved as 6/7 **SOME DATA LOSS***	OK, if 97-2000 Import Converter installed in 7.0 folder, or if 97 file saved as 6/7 **SOME DATA LOSS***	OK	OK	OK
	Word 97-2000 Viewer for Windows 3.x (free)	OK, VIEW ONLY **SOME DATA LOSS****	OK, VIEW ONLY **SOME DATA LOSS****	OK, VIEW ONLY **SOME DATA LOSS****	OK, VIEW ONLY **SOME DATA LOSS****	OK VIEW ONLY	OK VIEW ONLY	OK VIEW ONLY	VIEW ONLY	VIEW ONLY
	Word 6.0	OK, if 97-2000 Import Converter installed in 6.0 folder, or if 98 file saved as 6.0 **SOME DATA LOSS***	OK	OK **SOME DATA LOSS**	OK **SOME DATA LOSS**	OK, if 97-2000 Import Converter installed in 6.0 folder, or if '00 file saved as 6.0 **SOME DATA LOSS***	OK, if 97-2000 Import Converter installed in 6.0 folder, or if 97 file saved as 6.0 **SOME DATA LOSS***	OK	OK	OK
	Word 2.0	OK, if 98 file saved as 2.0 for Windows **SOME DATA LOSS****	OK, if 6.0/7.0 Import Converter installed, or if 6.0 file saved as 2.0 for Windows **SOME DATA LOSS****	OK, if 5.x file saved as 2.0 for Windows **SOME DATA LOSS****	OK **SOME DATA LOSS**	OK, if 2000 file saved in 2.0 format **SOME DATA LOSS***	OK, if 2000 file saved in 2.0 format **SOME DATA LOSS***	OK, if 6.0/7.0 Converter for Win 2.0 installed, or if 7.0 file saved in 2.0 format **SOME DATA LOSS****	OK, if 6.0/7.0 Converter for Win 2.0 installed, or if 6.0 file saved in 2.0 format **SOME DATA LOSS****	OK

*Because the file is being converted from 97-2000 to an older format, any special new features of Word 97-2000 are lost. E.g., there are over thirty features in the 97-2000 versions of Word that will not work. In the case of converting a 97-2000 file to the older 7.0 (or Word 95 or 6.0) format, lost features include: editing of charts, embedded True Type fonts, page borders, animated text formatting, graphics effects like embossed and engraved character formatting, document backgrounds, shadows, perspective, preset shaded fills, picture and textured backgrounds, use of .emf, .png & .jpg graphic formats (converted to .wmf and .pict), floating pictures, text box margins, text effects, embedded hyperlinks, and hyperlinks that combine Play Sound with other actions, as well as Title Master formatting changes, and editing of headers and footers, password protection, macros, and customized menu and toolbar settings. In the case of converting a 97-2000 file to the even older 4.0/5.x Macintosh or 2.0 for Windows formats, additional lost features include: variable width columns, page orientation, page size, and vertical alignment.

**6.0-specific features lost during conversion to 5.x or 2.0 for Windows include variable width columns, lines between columns, kerning, vertical alignment, automatic bullets and numbering, drawn objects, fields, revision marks, and master documents.

***The Word 97-2000 Viewer for Windows 3.1 does not support display of pictures contained in Word for Macintosh files.

Change the RAM (Memory) Allocated to *Word*

Word presentations with scanned pictures or movies need a lot of RAM. If you are using a Macintosh computer, it would be advisable to increase the amount of memory allocated to *Word* when you are creating or viewing files like these. Windows computers have another allocation method so this lesson refers only to Macintosh users. If you don't bump up the allocation, you will likely get the error message, "Memory was too full to draw everything." This doesn't mean that your computer doesn't have enough memory; it means that not enough of the memory has been allocated to *Word*.

Determining the Amount of RAM (Memory) Available

Before you bump up the allocation, you need to know how much memory is being used by your system and your screen saver.

1. To do this, choose "About This Computer" from the Apple menu in the left corner of your menu bar.

   The dialog box will tell you how much RAM (memory) is available on your computer and how much is being used by the system and the screen saver (DarkSide in this example).

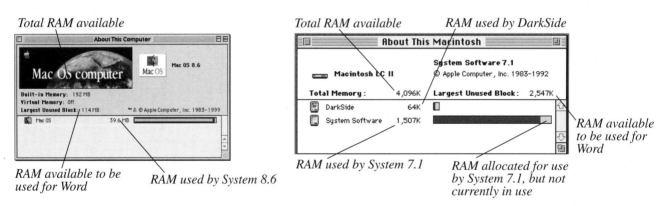

Total RAM available

Total RAM available   *RAM used by DarkSide*

RAM available to be used for Word

RAM available to be used for Word   *RAM used by System 8.6*

RAM used by System 7.1   *RAM allocated for use by System 7.1, but not currently in use*

Now that you know how much memory is available to be used for *Word*, it is time to see how much has been allocated for the program. Open the Microsoft Office folder.

2. Click once on the *Word* application icon to select it.

   If you click twice, the application will launch. The application must be closed to do this operation, so you must quit *Word* if it is open.

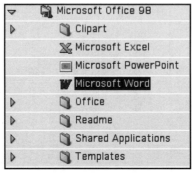

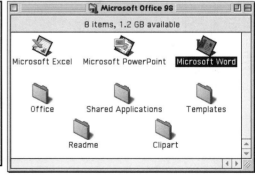

3. Once the application icon is selected (highlighted), choose Get Info, or press ⌘I. (If you have Mac OS 8 or higher you then need to choose Memory from the File menu.)

A dialog box will appear showing how much memory is needed for the application and how much has been allocated.

The System "About This Computer" dialog box shows that 122.6 megabytes of RAM could be used by *Word*. Don't use it all though.

Power Macintoshes

Word operates with less RAM on Power Macintoshes if Virtual Memory is turned on. Virtual Memory allocates a portion of the hard drive storage space as RAM (memory). Virtual Memory can be changed by opening Memory from the Control Panels.

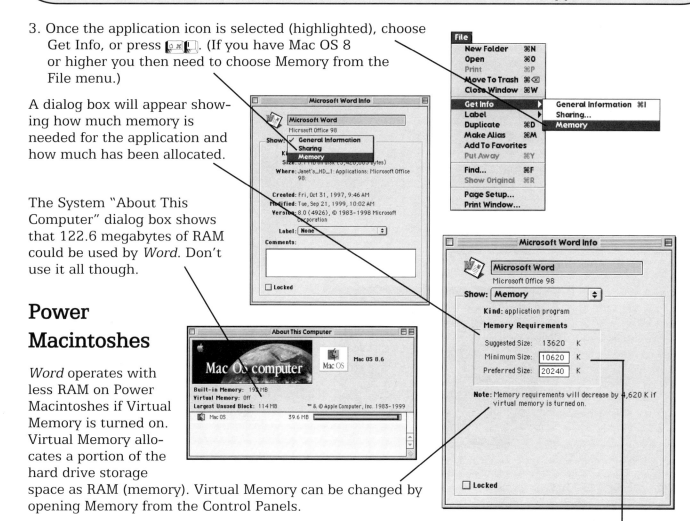

Changing the Amount of RAM Allocated to *Word*

1. Click in the boxes next to Preferred Size and Minimum Size and type a larger number.

2. Click the Close box in the upper left corner to close the window.

3. Open the *Word* program. Because you just allocated extra memory to the program, you will probably have enough memory to do most operations. If you get a memory error, save your file, quit *Word*, and allocate more memory (if available).

4. When you are finished with your work and have quit *Word*, you may need to change the memory allocation back to the suggested size. If you are working on your own computer and you frequently use large files in *Word*, you may decide to keep the allocation as you have set it.

You will not be able to have another program open at the same time you are using *Word* if all the available RAM is allocated to *Word*. If you keep your calendar program open throughout the day, as well as using *Word*, you may wish to take the memory allocation back to the suggested size so you can have them both open. If you are using a computer that is used by many people, it is advisable to change the allocation back to the suggested size and bump it up the next time you need to.

If you try to type a new number in the Preferred Size box and nothing happens, you probably have Word open. Quit Word and then you will be able to type in the dialog box.

Animals
Amphibians

Firebellied Toad

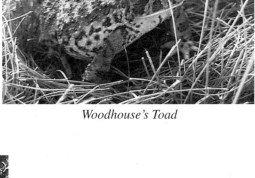

Tomato Frog

Gray Tree Frog

Woodhouse's Toad

Newt

Mud Puppy

Salamander in Nymph Stage

Basilisk

Tiger Salamander

Birds

Red-Winged Blackbird

Blue Jay

Western Bluebird

Gray Jay

Red-Bellied Woodpecker

Eastern Bluebird

Cardinal, Male

Cardinal, Female

House Finch

Black-Capped Chickadee

Gold Crown Sparrow

Robin

Crow

Western Meadowlark

Penguin

Pigeon

Hummingbird

Killdeer

Penguins

Ptarmigan

Pelican

Anhinga

Purple Gallinule

Flamingo

Roseate Spoonbill

Great Blue Heron

Great American Egret

White and Scarlet Ibis

Wood Stork

Seagull

Swan

Mallard, Female

Mallard, Male

Ring-Necked Pheasant

Red-Tailed Hawk

Sandhill Crane

Canada Goose

Chicken

Wild Turkey

Ostrich

Sharp-Tailed Grouse

Greater Prairie Chicken

Cockatoo

Scarlet Macaw

Yellow-Headed Parrot

Victoria Crowned Pigeon

Fish

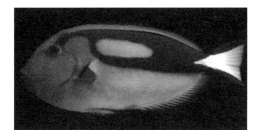

Hepatus Tang

Catfish

Clown Fish

Pompano

Grouper

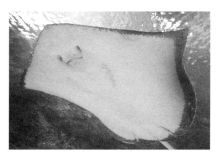

Stingray

Yellow Tang

Shark

Zoo Animals

Tapir

Tiger

Gorilla

Elephant

Giraffe

Mountain Lion

Lion

Marmoset

Polar Bear

Rhinoceros

Mammals

Elk2

Pronghorn

Moose

Deer

Elk

Elk

Bison

Mountain Sheep

Mountain Goat

Coyote

Rabbit

Raccoon2

Raccoon

Snowshoe Hare

Rodents

Muskrat

Pika

Guinea Pig

Fox Squirrel

Ground Squirrel

Fox Squirrel2

Marmot

Reptiles

Bearded Dragon

Rat Snake

Monitor Lizard

Turtles

Alligator

Insects

Bee

Hunter's Butterfly/American Painted Lady

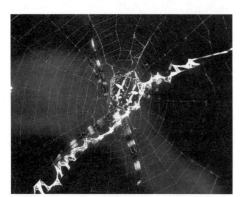

Spider

Dragonfly

Monarch Butterfly

Cloudless Sulphur

Pipevine Swallowtail

Eastern Swallowtail

Plants

Fruit, Berries, and Seeds

Apple Seeds

Apples

Raspberry

Dandelion Seeds

Evergreen Berries

Milkweed Seeds

Flowers

Rose

American Lotus

Purple Coneflower

Lily

Fireweed

Sneezeweed

Jack-in-the-Pulpit

Pasqueflower

Bird of Paradise

Hollyhock

Bougainvillea

Thistle

Siberian Iris

Columbine

Bachelor's Button

Water Lily

Water Lily2

Coneflower

Rose2

Goblin Gaillardia

Clematis

Mandevilla

Mushrooms

Graying Yellow Russula

Destroying Angel

Luminescent Panellus

Flecked-Flesh Polypore

Orange Pinwheel

Witches' Butter

Stalked Hairy Fairy Cup

Antler Jelly

Tree Volvariella

Blue Cheese Polypore

Common Morel

Lichen Agaric

Rosy Gomphidius

Shelf Mushroom

Cacti

Prickly Pear Cactus2

Arizona Hedgehog

Prickly Pear Cactus3

Barrel Cactus

Prickly Pear Cactus

Cholla & Saguaro Cacti

Notes:

Index

A

About This Computer 10
Alphabetize. *See* Sorting
Apple Menu 10
Application Icon 64, 97, 98
Application Menu 11
Arrowhead Lines 61
Assignment Sheet 67
AutoCorrect 38
   Adding an AutoCorrect Entry 38
   Apply As You Type 38
   Replace As You Type 39
Automatic Page Numbers 49
AutoShapes 54, 65
   Adding Multiple 66
   Changing the Color 66
   Creating a 3-D Shape 66
   Creating a Banner 65
   Creating a Shadowed Shape 66
   Creating an Arrow 65
   Drawing a Basic Shape 66
   Editing the AutoShape 54
   Formatting a 3-D Shape 66
   Rotating the Arrow 65
AutoText 74
   Closing 74
AutoText Toolbar 20

B

Boldfacing 28
Bookmark 96
Borders 52, 142
   Adding a Page Border 53
   Adding a Title Border 53
   Creating an AutoShapes Border 54
   Inserting a Graphic Border 54
   Paragraph Border 90
   Removing a Page Border 53
   Shading the Title 53
Boundaries
   Text Boundaries 92
Break
   Column Break 57
   Continuous 57
   Page 50
Breaks
   Inserting a Page Break 92
   Page Break 92
Brochure 91, 133

Bullets 55
Bullets and Numbering 55
   Customize 55
Button Help 17

C

Case of Text 41
   Lowercase 41
   Sentence Case 41
   Title Case 41
   Toggle Case 41
   Uppercase 41
Case of the Text 56
Clicking 4, 8
Clip Art 59, 82, 87
Column Boundaries 87
Column Break 57
Columns 57, 86, 92, 127
Comments 42
   Deleting 43
   Inserting 42
   Viewing 43
Control Toolbox Toolbar 22
Creating a Form 48
Creating a *Word* File 13
Custom Outline 79
Customize *Word* 35

D

Data Source 75
   Editing the Data Source 75
Database Toolbar 20
Date
   Inserting a Changing Date 50
   Inserting a Fixed Date 50
Date and Time 87
Different Versions of *Word* 3
Double-clicking 4, 8
Dragging 4, 8
Drawing Toolbar 21
Drop Cap 58, 143

E

Envelopes 73
   Delivery Address 73
   Envelope from a Letter 73

Merging to an Envelope 77
Return Address 73
Equation 51
Editing the Equation 51

F

Find
Find what 29
Font Size 61
Footnotes 71
Removing a Footnote 71
Format Painter 44
Formatting Text 25, 89
Bold 27
Center Text 27
Italics 25
Underline 26
Formatting Toolbar 19
Forms Toolbar 22
Frames Toolbar 22

G

Grammar 31, 32
Turning Off Automatic Grammar Checking 37
Group 87

H

Hanging Indent 29, 46
Headers/Footers 49, 118
Help on the Web 18
HTML 101
Hyperlinks
Bookmark 96
Creating a Graphic Hyperlink 96
Creating a Hyperlink within the Document 96
Creating a Text Hyperlink 95
Hyperlinking to *PowerPoint* 98
Hyperlinking to the Internet 97

I

Indenting 52
Indenting Text 29
Index 18
Inserting a Text Box 93
Internet 144, 145, 146, 147
Copying an Image 64
Create a Web Page 99
Hyperlinking to the Internet 97
Saving as HTML 101
Internet Pictures 64
Copying an Image 64

Downloading the Image 64
Pasting an Image 64

L

Labels 73
Launching the Program 13
Leader Tabs 47
Leading 72
Letterheads 81
Line Color 87
Linked Pages 95

M

Margins 28, 39, 81, 86
Changing 39
Math Worksheet 51
Merged Document 115
Completing the Main Document 76
Creating the Main Document 74
Creating a Mail Merge Document 74
Creating the Data Source 75
Editing the Data Source 75
Merging to an Envelope 77
Previewing the Merged Document 77
View Merged Document 77
Merged Letter 74
Microsoft Equation 51
Movie 62
Inserting 62
Playing 63

N

Newsletter 86
Creating 112
Non-Printing Characters 29, 40

O

Office Assistant 16
Opening a *Word* File 14
Opening Files 3
Outline 78
Creating a Shortcut 80
Creating Custom 79
Editing the Style 79
Outline View 78

P

Page Break 50
Page Numbers 49
Page Setup 91

Landscape 91
Picture 61, 93
    From File 61
    Inserting Digital Pictures 105, 114
    Internet 64
Picture Toolbar 22
Previewing the Document 26, 30
Printing 27
Printing a File 15

Q

Quotes 39

R

Replace
    Replace with 29
Reviewing Toolbar 22
Rubric 67

S

Saving 27
Saving a File 14
Saving Files 7, 11
Saving the File 27
    Saving as HTML 101
Screen Shots 84, 135
    Creating Arrowhead Lines 85
    Labeling the Screen Shot 85
Section Breaks 57
Sorting 56
Spell Check 31
    Document 31
    Single Word 31
Spelling 31
    Turning Off Automatic Spelling 37
Spelling and Grammar 31
Standard Toolbar 19

T

Tables 68, 111, 129, 139, 148
    Adding Clip Art 70
    Adding Text 68
    Distribute Rows Evenly 100
    Distributing the Columns & Rows 70
    Draw Table 100
    Drawing a Row 69
    Drawing the Table 70
    Entering Text 70
    Formatting the Table 100
    Insert Table 68
    Inserting Symbols 69

Setting Row Height 68
Tables & Borders Toolbar 22
Tabs 26, 28
    Center 45
    Decimal 45
    Leader 47
    Left 45
    Remove 45
    Right 45
Taskbar 5, 64, 97, 98
Template
    Saving As a Template 83, 88
    Using a Template 83
Text
    Bold 27
    Center 27
    Italics 25
    Justify Text 26
    Size 27
    Underline 26
Text Boundaries
    Column Boundaries 87
    Viewing 92
Text Box 60, 61, 81, 93
    Insert Clip Art 60
Text Boxes 113, 141, 145, 146, 147
Text Size
    Zoom Box 52
Thesaurus 34
3-D Settings Toolbar 22
3-D Toolbar 22
Toolbars 19
    3-D Settings Toolbar 22
    3-D Toolbar 22
    Adding Buttons 35
    AutoText Toolbar 20
    Control Toolbox Toolbar 22
    Creating New 36
    Customize 35
    Database Toolbar 20
    Drawing Toolbar 21
    Formatting Toolbar 19
    Forms Toolbar 22
    Frames Toolbar 22
    Picture Toolbar 22
    Removing Buttons 36
    Reviewing Toolbar 22
    Standard Toolbar 19
    Tables & Borders Toolbar 22
    Viewing 37
    Visual Basic Toolbar 21
    Web Toolbar 20
    WordArt Toolbar 20

V

View Merged Document
   Viewing Records 77
Visual Basic Toolbar 21

W

Watermark 89
Web Page 99
Web Toolbar 20
Wizard 30
   Resume Wizard 30
WordArt 69, 82, 87
   Formatting the WordArt 69
WordArt Toolbar 20
Wrapping 59
   In front of 60
   In line with 60
   Square 59, 88
   Through 60
   Tight 59
   Top & Bottom 60
Wrapping Text 46

Z

Zoom Box 52

Notes:

Tom Snyder Productions®

80 Coolidge Hill Road • Watertown, MA 02472-5003 • USA
Phone 1-800-342-0236 • Fax 1-800-304-1254 • www.tomsnyder.com

XJAN POW U 02